Jane Newdick & Neil Sutherland

FLOWER ARRANGING

Photography by
NEIL SUTHERLAND

Text and arrangements by
JANE NEWDICK

with additional material by
DEE HINE
PETER SNARE
ELIZABETH PALMER
TRICIA HALL

Design
Bridgewater Design Ltd

Commissioning
Trevor Hall
Hanni Penrose
Andrew Preston

Editorial
Fleur Robertson
Gill Waugh

Production
Gerald Hughes
Ruth Arthur

Director of Publishing
David Gibbon

CLB 2025
© 1989 Colour Library Books Ltd, Godalming, Surrey, England.
All rights reserved.
This 1989 edition published by Portland House, a division of dilithium Press Ltd,
distributed by Crown Publishers, Inc, 225 Park Avenue South, New York, New York 10003.
Typesetting by Words and Spaces, Hampshire, England.
Colour separations by Hong Kong Graphic Arts Ltd, Hong Kong.
Produced in England.
ISBN 0-517-68027-0
h g f e d c b a

Library of Congress Cataloging-in-Publication Data
Newdick, Jane.
    Flower arranging/Jane Newdick and Neil Sutherland.
    p. cm.
    ISBN 0-517-68027-0
    1. Flower arrangement. I. Sutherland, Neil. II Title.
SB449.N37 1989
745.92—dc19   89-3706
                        CIP

Jane Newdick & Neil Sutherland
FLOWER ARRANGING

PORTLAND HOUSE

CONTENTS

INTRODUCTION

LOWERS HAVE VERY SPECIAL QUALITIES that make them unique in nature. We respond to them very directly as they affect our senses profoundly through their colour, scent and texture and their quite breathtaking variety of shapes.

A house without flowers or plants, however beautifully furnished and decorated, is somehow not welcoming and friendly. Bringing about this transformation does not require bunches of expensive, out-of-season flowers, elaborate containers and hours of time and skill. It takes no time to buy or pick a pretty bunch of blooms to stand in a kitchen jug or pretty vase, and by this simple process you have added colour, vibrancy, and the chance to watch a living thing change and open, look perfect for a few days then gently fade.

In this book you will find ideas for every kind of flower arrangement you might like to make, from the simplest to the very grand. Between the two there are ideas for special occasions and celebrations, everyday kinds of arrangements and specialised flowers such as herbs, or stricter arranging methods such as Ikebana. You may be a first-time flower arranger who needs to learn everything from the beginning, or a skilled flower arranger who would like some new ideas and fresh inspiration. The practical section at the front of the book sets out to guide you through choosing equipment, caring for and conditioning flowers as well as providing guidelines for such things as colour scheming and lighting flowers. The second part of the book offers page after page of stunning pictures of different flowers to show as much as possible of the materials available either to grow or buy.

The flower arranger with a garden has a definite advantage, as it is possible to grow wonderful flowers and also foliage, which just isn't available to buy. However, the supply of flowers grown commercially now improves every year, with adventurous growers trying new species and varieties to offer to the trade.

Even small flower shops these days can offer a selection greater than a few types of rose, carnation and chrysanthemum, and the more people ask for unusual, interesting flowers the more these will become available. Meanwhile, if you have a little extra space in a garden, do plant some flowers specially for cutting, and sow a few easy and quick annual seeds for picking through the summer months. A good way of growing flowers for picking is to treat them like a vegetable crop and sow them in rows. This makes them easier to cultivate, water and pick than if they were scattered amongst ordinary garden plants.

The history of flower arranging has not been very well documented down the ages, possibly because flowers are often taken for granted. We can assume that they have been used as decoration for as long as man has been on this planet, and they have made, and still do make, important contributions to festivals, celebrations, religious occasions, weddings, christenings and funerals. They are often used to convey messages which are too difficult to put into words, and at one time there was an elaborate language and symbolism of flowers which was both sophisticated and subtle.

Looking at historic interiors from, say, the seventeenth or nineteenth centuries, we can almost imagine the types of flowers and styles of arrangements the owners would have preferred. These days we have very eclectic taste and more or less anything goes. People do still want formal, large and elaborate arrangements for special occasions and grand interiors, but the mood for the last years of the twentieth century in flowers is one of simplicity, naturalness and a relaxed and easy feel to fit in with most people's lives.

Finally, remember that there are no rules to flower arranging and that it isn't a competition to use the most flowers in the most contrived positions. Simply get together some flowers in colours you love, treat them with care and respect and just have fun. The materials will speak for themselves, and you can't help but achieve a perfect flower arrangement every time.

SECTION 1

A Practical Guide

CHAPTER 1

CHOOSING MATERIALS AND EQUIPMENT

INTRODUCTION

K NOWING WHAT EQUIPMENT and materials are needed for a new craft and which are the best types to buy can be difficult. Flower arranging, luckily, requires just a few basic tools to start, though it is useful to have an awareness of what is available for any special projects that might be undertaken.

Many people will find that they already have the necessary things if they own a garden or run a kitchen. If you intend to put together some fairly complicated arrangements or any on a grand scale then you will need to know the professional tricks for keeping flowers fresh and supported in containers and the products available to help you do this.

None of this equipment is very costly, and most things are re-useable. If you have enough space it makes sense to keep everything needed for flower arranging in one place near where you will work. Try to be firm about using cutting tools only for flower arranging and don't let them be used for household purposes. Sharp tools are a must but can easily be blunted by using them on unsuitable materials, so if there is any chance of this happening, keep them hidden away. Keep steel wires somewhere dry and wrapped in oiled paper as they rust very quickly in damp conditions. The rust won't hurt but it makes the wires dirty and unpleasant to use.

If you are working on flower arrangements away from home, make up a portable tool kit to keep in a light tool box, or else a fabric wrap with pockets in which to slot all the tools, rolls of wire

Facing page: a selection of the materials and equipment needed to make dried flower arrangements. Foam is available in a special form for dried work in a subtle grey-brown colour and in many different shapes. Stiff lengths of stub wire are used on flowers which have weak stems, and softer rose wire is ideal for fixing flower heads or leaves to a stem or wire.

Above: a collection of dried and preserved autumn flowers and foliage with a simple country feel. The beech leaves, molucella and fatsia leaves have been preserved in glycerine, which gives them a soft, bronzey-brown shine. In contrast, brilliant orange physalis lanterns and golden yellow achillea glow warmly in a plain and simple setting.

and bits and pieces. When dry, floral foam can be crumbly and vulnerable, so store it in a cardboard box, or at least keep odd blocks in plastic bags. Any left-over bits which are damp should be wrapped in plastic and stored for another time.

Finally, consider where you will be working with flowers. Small and simple arrangements are easily put together in one place and moved afterwards, but larger, more complicated ones will need to be made in situ. For those arrangements invest in a cloth or sheet of plastic to catch any bits and protect furnishings. An ideal place to work is in a utility room or in the kitchen near water and on practical work surfaces.

SCISSORS AND SECATEURS

WHICH TOOLS YOU CHOOSE to work with will depend on the kind of flower arranging that you do, and on what you find comfortable to use. A pair of scissors or secateurs is vital for cutting stems. Some people prefer to use a small pair of florists' scissors rather than secateurs as these can be heavy to use for long. While most flowers are easily cut with good scissors there will be times when you need to cut woody tree or shrub stems, and then secateurs are required. If you only intend to buy one cutting tool, a good pair of secateurs is probably the best choice and, for anyone with small hands, it is possible to find very well made ones on a small scale.

The scissors sold specially for flower arranging have short, wide blades with blunt ends and lightweight handles. These short blades makes it easy to nip out small leaves and stems from amongst a lot of plant material, and many versions have serrated blades for cutting through tough stems and through wire, which would blunt normal blades.

There are some very specialised scissors on the market which also incorporate a device to crush and clean stems of thorns or small leaves. Some of these tools take some getting used to so it is probably better to keep to a simple, straightforward version to begin with. There are some beautiful Japanese scissors available designed for ikebana and Japanese-style arrangements.

KNIVES

A SMALL CRAFT KNIFE is occasionally useful for paring or cutting stems without crushing them. You will need a knife to cut blocks of floral foam, but for this purpose any long-bladed kitchen knife will do well enough, and it does not need to be particularly sharp.

FLORAL FOAM

FLORAL FOAM is a very useful product for the flower arranger as it facilitates all kinds of creative possibilities. It isn't always necessary, and in some cases it would be wrong to use it in simple arrangements, yet it is something that you are bound to want to experiment with. Known and sold under various trade names such as Oasis and Florapack, it comes in basic rectangular blocks which can be cut for all shapes of container. Made from a special expanded foam which readily absorbs water, it holds flowers firmly (as long as they are not too heavy) and it keeps them in good condition, though the container will still need to be topped up with water every now and again. Floral foam also comes in shapes

Above: an explosion of early summer blooms arranged in a classic terracotta urn. The mix of so many different colours works as so many different varieties of flowers have been used. Lilies, irises, roses and delphiniums mingle with scabious, zinnias, poppies and sweet peas. Many garden flowers and annuals are included.

*op right: some of the equipment needed for flower arranging. While
 is not neccessary to have many accessories, a few essential tools,
such as scissors and secateurs, are vital for good work. The green
oam comes in basic blocks which can be cut smaller, and in a few
special, smaller shapes.*

designed for specific plastic trays, and wreath bases pre-filled with foam are available. The foam designed to be used wet usually comes in green, but there is also a dry version which is brown for use in dried flower arrangements.

Floral foams absorb water in seconds rather than minutes, and so are quick and easy to use. Remember, though, not to over soak them as they can become crumbly and will fall apart if too many stems are put into them or if the arrangement is altered too many times. Soak foam in just off-cold rather than freezing-cold water, which flowers do not enjoy. Foam can be taped to a base, squeezed inside a container or fixed onto special pins. In some large containers it will be necessary to use floral foam with rumpled wire mesh over the top of it to support large stems. Blocks of foam can be built up for large scale arrangements, but these will dry out quickly unless the base block is sitting in a reservoir of water. Complicated structures such as swags can be made using small chunks of foam sandwiched between wire mesh with each piece of foam wrapped in plastic film to retain the moisture.

WIRE MESH

IN THE DAYS BEFORE floral foam was available the only support for flower stems, apart from pin holders, was crumpled wire mesh. Wired over the top of a container or squeezed into the neck of a vase it held stems steady, albeit somewhat stiffly. People still like to use it these days as it is cheap and re-useable. It is possible to buy plastic coated mesh which is clean and doesn't scratch containers, but in most cases ordinary chicken wire is fine and usually easier to bend and manipulate. When using wire mesh remember not to crumple it so tightly that not enough holes and spaces are left for stems to be pushed through. Aim at roughly three layers of wire in the container with the holes as evenly spaced as possible. Once the wire is in a vase it can be left there, although you will obviously need to remove stains and debris sometimes.

Don't be tempted to cut wire with flower scissors or secateurs (unless they have a special facility for doing this) as the blades will quickly get blunted. Keep any surplus wire mesh rolled up in a dry place to prevent it from rusting.

A tall and potentially top-heavy arrangement benefits from crumpled wire or a pin holder in the vase.

REEL WIRE AND STUB WIRE

ANOTHER TYPE OF WIRE commonly used in floristry is thin, strong and very malleable wire often sold on a reel and cut to length as required. It is used for all kinds of purposes, whenever anything needs to be tied. For example, to secure wire mesh in position round the neck of a container, to hang wire-covered foam shapes into position or to fix vases to pedestals. Thinner rose wire is very useful for tying small bunches of flowers together or stiffening small stems for formal bouquets. It is usually bright, shiny silver, though it is possible to get dark brown wire, which is better camouflaged in dried flower arrangements. Rose wire is sometimes sold in small packs of pre-cut lengths, but is more use on a reel in case you need long pieces of it. Rose wire can be used in the fixing of stiff stub wires to flower heads or stems and also to make tiny, U-shaped pins for keeping some flower heads, such as roses, from opening, and for wiring small, decorative leaves into bouquets where the leaf's own stem would be too clumsy. The average flower arranger may not need rose wire, which is very fiddly to work, but it is useful to know its uses.

Stub wires are stiff wires available in several different thicknesses and lengths. Usually sold in packs of one size they are also available in much larger bundles sold by weight — again all in one thickness. They can be cut to the length you require with wire cutters or special scissors and are used to support sagging flower stems. Nowadays they are used much more commonly for dried flowers. Certain flowers such as helichrysums are wired onto stub wires soon after picking to replace their very feeble stems. Flower heads that have been dried in desiccants are put onto wires and small bunches of flowers such as cornflowers can be wired onto a thick stub wire and positioned in an arrangement. For general, day-to-day flower arrangements stub wires won't often be needed, but if you are thinking of making a lot of dried arrangements then it is a good idea to buy a large stub-wire bundle. This type of wire rusts easily so keep it wrapped in oiled paper.

PIN HOLDERS

THESE HEAVY DEVICES FOR ANCHORING STEMS are not used very much these days. They were perfect for fairly loose, open arrangements in a wide-necked container or to add some security to long-stemmed, woody branches. The heavy base often had lead set into it to make it steady and the top surface was made up of sharp spikes or pins. The flower stems are stuck onto and between these pins. There is another type of holder often made from glass which is covered with holes and again this is designed to sit at the bottom of a container and keep stems in place. They can be tricky

Large and elaborate arrangements will need frequent topping up with water from a long-spouted watering can.

to use, but are sometimes helpful for stiff, small stems, such as those on sweet peas, making it possible to arrange a whole mass of these in a shallow bowl with space round each individual bloom − something difficult to do any other way.

It is possible to buy strips of adhesive (rather like putty) which can be used to secure pin holders and other devices in place inside a container.

WATERING CANS AND SPRAYS

MOST PEOPLE MAKE DO with a jug or kettle to fill containers with water yet proper watering cans cost very little and reduce the risk of spilling or splashing water onto polished furniture or fabrics. A can with a long, thin spout is ideal because it can be directed right into the middle of an arrangement or onto floral foam precisely where the water is needed. Flowers standing in a warm room will need to be topped up with water once a day, so an efficient can is essential.

A spray or mister is not imperative but again can be useful in hot, dry weather or in over-heated rooms. A fine mist of cool water perks up many flowers, almost visibly refreshing them. A few varieties, such as violets and hydrangeas, actually take up water through their petals, so a fine spray of water can revive these flowers wonderfully.

TAPES, STEM WRAP AND RIBBONS

IN THE MORE SPECIALISED branches of floristry, such as the construction of formal wedding bouquets and posies, flower stems are often wired for support or replaced by wires, and these in turn are wrapped in a special tape which clings to the stem or wire and to itself, sealing out air and holding in moisture. These tapes are nowadays made from thin, stretchy plastic but were at one time made from gutta percha. They come in various colours, such as white, green and brown; for normal use the green seems to be the least obtrusive colour.

Also available are strong adhesive tapes which attach floral foam to plastic bases or any container; these come in various widths and most commonly in green, but also in white and brown. A roll of this tape about a centimetre wide is probably the most useful to have for normal work.

If you want to add bows to bouquets or posies you can either use fabric ribbons or the cheaper polyester ribbons sold specifically for floristry work. As you are unlikely to be using great quantities of ribbon it is worthwhile buying proper dressmakers' ribbons as these come in good colours and have a soft feel and drape.

CHAPTER 2

VASES AND CONTAINERS

INTRODUCTION

I N A SUCCESSFUL FLOWER ARRANGEMENT the flowers should, in general, be the focus of attention, though the container in which they are arranged can be very important to the overall effect. It is perfectly possible to arrange a group of flowers straight into floral foam without any kind of container at all, and this method is particularly useful for decorating large spaces, such as a church for a wedding, or when you need dozens of decorations and do not have enough similar-sized containers in which to put them.

The right choice of vase, basket, jug or whatever can provide a key part of the arrangement. A container may be the starting point or inspiration for an arrangement — or it may even be the

Facing page top: one of the simplest and plainest-shaped containers is also one of the most useful for the flower arranger. Here white aquilegia and Solomon's seal look sculptural mixed with hosta leaves, rhubarb flowers and cow parsley in a clear glass vase.

Facing page bottom: a variety of clear glass containers in sizes suitable for the tallest stems or the tiniest posies. Several of these vases would make a good basis for containers for the flower arranger who prefers simple-looking flowers.

Make use of containers that you already have, such as these miniature antique bottles (above). Here they have been used to hold one or two blooms of sweetly scented flowers such as honeysuckle, violas, old-fashioned roses, nicotiana and clematis.

A solid, straight, thick glass cylinder is the perfect container for tall-stemmed, important flowers such as pure white gladioli, greenish-white anemones and crisp gerbera daisies (left). In an arrangement like this the stems become as important as the flowers above, so keep them clean and foliage free.

Heavy-headed dahlias (above) look marvellous, but often have weak , flimsy stems. A handful or two of glass marbles at the bottom of a container will hold the stems in place and add more stability to the arrangement. The deep burgundy and white flowers contrast with greyish-green eucalyptus foliage and the saw-edged leaf of Hellebore corsicus.

Flowers of one variety often look good cut to one length and placed in a plain glass tank with their heads just above the rim of the container. This is one of the easiest types of arrangement to do and takes very little skill to achieve a superb effect. Left: here brilliant yellow daffodils have been used, but the idea works with many different types of flowers. This kind of arrangement looks good on a low table or windowsill where the colour and texture of the blooms can be appreciated from close up.

All kinds of containers make suitable vases for holding flowers. Most households will have a collection of glasses, which could include straight-sided tumblers or stemmed wine or liqueur glasses, all of which make very suitable vases for small-scale posies of flowers. A chunky glass goblet (right) has been used here to hold a delicate mixture of flowers in subtle blues, mauves and cream. There are Michaelmas daisies, anemones, love-in-a-mist, rue foliage and the lacey white flowers of dill.

If you have plenty of space for an arrangement, try grouping a collection of containers together. The tall glass vase in the centre (below) is perfectly balanced by the two smaller glasses either side and all three are linked by the simple white and green colour scheme of the flowers. The small glass holds anemones, chincherinchees and caraway flowers. The large vase is simply filled with caraway and the glass jelly mould contains tiny white daisies, Alchemilla mollis leaves, asparagus foliage and variegated euphorbia.

focal point, the flowers simply adding to its appeal. The colour of a container may be used to contrast with that of the flowers inside it or to echo it. Many people have favourite containers which they always use in one particular place in the house, such as in a small alcove, on a mantel shelf or on the kitchen table. Sometimes it is almost as if the vase or jug or whatever it is has become part of the furniture, simply decorated differently from week to week and through the seasons.

If you enjoy filling your house with flowers then you will always be on the look-out for new containers for your collection. Sales and secondhand shops are a good source — never scorn pieces with blemishes or chips missing as these can always be disguised with the flowers. It is a good idea to have a basic selection of a few very different containers for day-to-day arrangements. Jugs of all sizes are very useful for informal bunches and posies, and can be ceramic, or made of metal or glass. One or two clear glass tanks and a spherical fish bowl shape are perfect for crisp, stylish arrangements of single colour bunches, or arrangements where the stems are an important part of the overall look. A classic ceramic vase, perhaps on a stem, would be useful for formal arrangements, and a modern-style container or two in glass or a good plain colour would be suitable when you only have a few stems to arrange.

To this basic selection you could add extra items as and when you needed them. A few very small glasses for single blooms and miniature arrangements would be useful, as would a collection of baskets, both new and old, for country-style arrangements and dried flowers. Copper and brass and other metals such as pewter seem to be slightly out of fashion at the moment, but can look good, especially with autumnal oranges, reds and browns, though such heavy metals can dominate arrangements if you do not take great care.

CERAMIC AND GLASS

THE TYPE OF CONTAINERS YOU CHOOSE will obviously relate to the house you live in: if you have large rooms and plenty of space you will need some big vases for special occasions, whereas a small house with little rooms and no large pieces of furniture will need neat and unobtrusive containers for flowers. You need not think only in terms of vases for flowers, because all kinds of things make excellent containers: china tea pots, jugs and cups and saucers, plain or patterned, are very decorative filled with flowers. Some highly decorated pieces may well not work very well with elaborate arrangements, but certain designs always look good, such as tiny, all-over prints or blue-and-white patterns.

Glass jugs, wineglasses and bowls meant for serving food can all be put to good use and filled with flowers. A stemmed wineglass filled with a tiny posy makes a pretty table decoration beside each place setting. Bottles both old and new can look

Facing page: a collection of many types of container, including silver, glass, porcelain and earthenware, that any house might be able to provide.

Above: unlikely things sometimes make perfect containers for special flowers. A small mahogany tea caddy is used to show off tiny violas and pansies which are standing in water in small glass jars inside the box.

The kitchen can often provide a wonderful assortment of containers for flowers. Right: this shiny tin jelly mould looks stunning with the brilliant hot colours of a mixed bunch of gerbera daisies cut short and arranged thickly to make a beautiful table centrepiece.

A simple, uncompromising shape of vase needs just the right treatment. Above: the curving blades of bear grass perfectly echo the outline of the coral ceramic globe, and the warm pink gerberas have a simple, sculptured quality to them which is in tune with the overall shape of the arrangement. A vase this shape needs bold flowers and uncluttered lines to look right.

Left: a modern black glass vase in a distinctly Thirties shape. The flowers need to be dramatic to compete with its bold style. Here it has been filled with yellow chillies, orange rose hips and golden chrysanthemums. The grasses soften the effect and broaden the overall outline without spoiling the proportions.

Facing page: simple shapes and strong colours can be found in both old vases and modern versions.

stunning with just a few shapely branches inside, though the very narrow neck obviously limits what is possible. Strong, dark-coloured glass and china are lovely for bold, modern arrangements, but choose shapes which are well proportioned and not at all fussy if the colour is very dominant.

Old pieces of china and porcelain may be too precious to be in everyday use for flowers, but there are still plenty of slightly damaged or not very valuable old pieces which can be put to use. The soft, faded colours and elegant designs of many old pieces give you a head start before you add any flowers, while jugs in glass and china are one of the most useful containers for any flower arranger. They can be any size, from enormous water or milk pitchers to tiny cream jugs, their wide neck and comfortable, often round, shapes making them ideal for all types of arrangements. Many jugs come in sumptuous colours and patterns which add to an arrangement, but still their simple, homely purpose ensures that they are subordinate to the flowers.

A flower vase invites a certain formality in the design that you create, while plain, straight-sided cylinders and tanks are merely a device to hold water, and the flowers they contain are always simple and unarranged. You will need to decide what type of arrangement you are most likely to want, and buy and collect containers accordingly. Very often a group of more than one container makes a better statement than a solitary vase. For example you could stand a large vase behind a shorter, squat jug and beside the jug place a cup and saucer. The container colours should all relate, though the flower colours could be different in each container. If groups of containers don't suit a formal room arrangement, use pairs of matching containers or march a line

of small bowls or glasses all in the same shape along a table or mantel shelf.

Keep glass and china scrupulously clean and stored safely when not in use. Any really stubborn stains inside a vase can be removed by leaving a very weak solution of bleach in them over night.

SILVER

THERE IS NO DOUBT that the high shine of silver has a very special quality which is enhanced by the colours and textures of flowers. It is possible to find modern silver shapes, but generally silver vases will be traditional, even period pieces — a fact to bear in mind when choosing the style of flowers. Once rose bowls were frequently made in silver and stood empty as a decoration in their own right. Filled with full-blown summer roses they can look spectacular. Another common silver shape is a tall, thin flute designed to hold one or two perfect blooms. Immensely elegant, a vase like this demands a beautiful lily, orchid or rose.

Silver candlesticks are often used as stands for table or buffet decorations. You can either dispense with a candle and simply build an arrangement onto foam fixed across the candle cup, or you can keep a candle inside the stick and fix a ring of foam round its base. The ring is then filled with small and dainty flowers and foliage which can, if you like, trail down towards the table for a very romantic look. Try pink candles in a silver candlestick surrounded by miniature pink roses and pale, grey-green foliage. A word of warning, though — if water and flowers are left in silver for very long they can mark the interior, and care must be taken with wire mesh, which could scratch a finely polished surface.

Baskets in every size and material are very useful to the flower arranger. Their texture seems to have a natural affinity with fresh and dried flowers, and always makes the best of them. They can be lined with plastic or with metal foil and used with blocks of damp foam, or they can simply be used as a cache pot to cover the actual container which holds water and flowers. This enormous French shopping basket has been filled with sprays of wild hedgerow Queen Anne's Lace to disguise an empty summer hearth.

Make the most of summer fruits and vegetables and use them for instant waterproof containers. A small pumpkin, melon or squash can be hollowed out to make enough room for flower stems and then filled with water and flowers. Pare a little from the the base of the fruit first to be sure that it stands evenly and flat on the ground. These rustic containers look wonderful filled with simple summer flowers such as pot marigolds in shades of orange and yellow (left). Below: a prettily marked round courgette.

COPPER AND BRASS

IN THE PAST these cheaper metals have been made up into all kinds of containers, among them jugs and urns which are very suitable for holding flowers. These may have soldered joints however, so check that there aren't any leaks and, if in doubt, line the inside with plastic or metal foil and use floral foam, or stand a smaller container filled with water inside the metal one. Again, copper and brass will need to be cleaned and polished, unless they are lacquered, as in a damp atmosphere they quickly dull and go black.

The yellow tone of brass works well with creams, yellows and greens while the warmer, richer copper colour looks lovely with reds, plums, burnt oranges and mahogany browns.

PEWTER

ALTHOUGH PEWTER APPEARS to have little life of its own, it can look surprisingly good against many flowers. The deep grey of the metal is lovely with pinks and mauves and grey greens, as well as off-setting white or cream flowers. Simple, strong, old-fashioned pieces such as jugs and tankards demand very bold shapes and uncluttered lines. For example, a deep, pewter dish containing a bloom or two of highly scented magnolia grandiflora with their enormous shiny green and bronze leaves has a dignity and purity reminiscent of another age.

BASKETS

THE POPULARITY OF BASKETS as containers for flowers has really developed over the last few years, and nowadays baskets are imported from all over the world for this purpose. Most of them probably end up being used for dried flowers (to which end they are ideally suited), but don't underestimate their usefulness for fresh arrangements too. They can be lined with metal foil or plastic — in fact some are sold pre-lined with plastic — and then used with floral foam. If this is too fiddly or not suitable for the flowers you are using then simply stand a container of water inside the basket and fix it firmly with florists' adhesive.

A small and dainty piece of china (top left), shaped like the leaves of a cabbage, is a suitable vase for a pretty apricot and peach mixture of spray carnations, honeysuckle, roses and unusual snippets of berries and leaves from the garden. This kind of arrangement is easiest to put together using floral foam taped into the vase.

A teapot might not be the obvious choice of container for flowers, but this brilliant, shiny, scarlet pot (above) was exactly right to show off a garden bunch of Shirley poppies, geraniums, sweet peas and marigolds. The shape of a teapot restricts what is possible in terms of arranging, but a straightforward bunch or a posy of flowers works well.

Most baskets come in a variation of brown, cream or ginger, but they can be quickly and easily sprayed or sponged any colour you choose, or stained in more subtle colours with inks or wood stains. The rustic, earthy feel of a basket invariably enhances plant materials, giving an air of informality. It would be hard to make a highly sophisticated arrangement in a basket, but they do have the advantage of slotting into any situation with ease, looking quite at home both on an elegant piece of antique furniture or a scrubbed wood work surface. Whether you choose a basket with a handle is up to you: arranging the flowers can be a little harder if there is a handle to consider, but a handle may also add a rather pleasing finishing touch or become an important piece of the design.

WOOD

WHILE THERE ARE FEW WOODEN PIECES made specially for use as flower containers, there are plenty of things which can be put to that use, such as salad bowls, tea caddies, writing boxes, spice boxes, woodchip fruit baskets and miniature chests, for example. They will have to be lined and made waterproof in some way and a secondary container put in place to hold water. Use simple flowers that do not look too contrived if they are in an unlikely container.

BITS AND PIECES

ALL MANNER OF THINGS can be pressed into use to display flowers, so always be on the look out. Decorative tins and cans which once contained oils, olives, or biscuits can have the lid removed and the inside cleaned. Some plastic containers are stylish when emptied of their product, while entirely unlikely shops such as an ironmonger's can produce a galvanised paint can or terracotta flower pot which — with a bit of imagination — can become a stylish flower container.

You can use fruit and vegetables or even a hollowed out loaf of bread as short term containers. A melon or squash scooped out and emptied can be filled with water safely and large leafy vegetables such as cabbages can have flowers added to them or arranged inside the hollowed-out centre. Smaller fruits, such as apples or peppers, make bright and colourful vases and, while they will not stay perfect for more than a few days, make lovely instant decorations for parties or table settings. Further interesting containers are likely to be found in any kitchen. Bright, shiny metal moulds and cake tins make perfect places for flowers, especially bunches of strongly coloured, simple flowers such as daisies and gerbera. Old glass and china jelly moulds are good too, having simple outlines and interesting surfaces. Jam pots and glass bottles, egg cups and casseroles — all of these seen in a different light from their usual everyday role means that most households have dozens of containers permanently to hand. The garden too offers all kinds of opportunities. Terracotta pots are cheap and effective (though of course they have to be lined or used with an inner container), while garden trugs and baskets give an instant country feel to any arrangement. Other possibilities include watering cans and stone or plastic urns and pots, as well as hanging baskets for suspended arrangements.

CHAPTER 3

FLOWER SOURCES

INTRODUCTION

A FLOWER-FILLED GARDEN with plenty of blooms available is a dream for many people. The reality may be a city apartment or small back yard with no space to grow anything and entirely the wrong conditions in which even to try. Yet most of us have access to flowers from a market stall or flower shop, a hedgerow or garden. This chapter sets out to explain which flowers you can find where, and how to get the best on offer at a reasonable price. If you are fortunate enough to have some land to cultivate then it is definitely worth growing species for cutting. Years ago, large country houses, always had a section of kitchen garden kept for growing blooms for the house, and material would be taken from there every day — even in the

depths of winter, when hot house flowers and potted plants had to stand in for summer blossoms.

Even if you have quite a small garden there are a few plants which look good growing but which can be picked for indoors as well. Some of the winter-scented flowering shrubs would make a good choice, as would a hydrangea for flower heads to dry. A small patch or row of some of the easy hardy annuals such as cornflowers and larkspur would give flowers to pick right through the summer months. If you already grow fruit and vegetables then it is little extra trouble to grow a few flowers alongside them.

The commercial flower market these days is enormous and world wide. It seems that there is very little which cannot be obtained now at any time throughout the year; one can even buy tulips in November and chrysanthemums in May, and there is

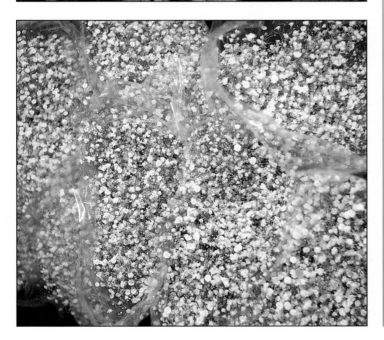

A good flower shop (facing page) will have an enormous range of flowers for sale, with many varieties to choose from and a good colour range. As well as cut flowers, most shops sell foliage, dried and artificial flowers and both flowering and foliage pot plants. If the flowers are well displayed it can be a great inspiration to the customer, while flowers arranged in colour groups make choosing blooms very much easier.

Top left: wraps of fresh carnations waiting for a customer at a big wholesale market.

Smaller spray carnations (centre left) come in a wonderful range of colours and seem to be available all the year round. They are very popular as they are particularly long lived as a cut flower.

Bottom left: huge bunches of gypsophila, which is a very useful florists' filler and is sometimes dried. Traditionally used in bridal work, it adds a soft, fluffy effect to any arrangement.

Large wholesale flower markets (above) sell most of the flowers which appear in stalls and shops throughout the country. Flowers are flown in from all over the world to the daily week-day market, which begins in the very early hours of the morning and finishes with the floor space practically empty.

A garden of your own means that you can grow and pick exactly the flowers that you want to use. A sheltering wall is superb for climbing plants and anything which is a little delicate and tender. A brilliant scarlet climbing rose scrambles up this old stone wall, while lush clumps of peonies grow at its foot.

A garden provides scent and visual pleasure, as well as food for insects (top).

Above: the abundance of flowers available for the arranger in midsummer in this garden includes roses, catmint, Alchemilla mollis, and the soft, furry grey leaves of Stachys lanata.

a constant supply of new varieties appearing in the flower shops. Helped along by magazine features, television programmes, films and books, people have become used to seeing flowers used decoratively in every kind of interior, and they are willing to buy flowers more often and in every variety. The idea of a stiff arrangement in an old-fashioned vase is fading and we are prepared to see flowers as a statement of colour, fashion or style that says something about ourselves and how we want an environment to be. In big cities, flower retailers are responding quickly, aiming to sell bunches of flowers along with clothes or furniture or with the weekly groceries. Regionally, smaller florists still aim at the person coming to order a bouquet for delivery, or a ready-made arrangement for a hospital bedside. In Europe there is a long history of flowers being bought as gifts and thanks for hospitality, and as they become more widely available at a price most people can afford, flowers will become a normal part of every home.

BUYING FROM SHOPS AND MARKETS

A TYPICAL FLOWER SHOP THESE DAYS will have on offer flowers from all over the world. While home grown flowers are obviously cheaper and near to hand, most people want to see some of the more exotic varieties and tropical blooms as well. In Europe, Holland has become one of the biggest and busiest flower growers,

sending flowers to all the big markets. Generally speaking, flowers are sold by the grower to a wholesaler who sells on to flower shops and other retail outlets. It is possible in London's Nine Elms wholesale flower market for the general public to buy, but in most cases the obligation to buy very large quantities and the exceedingly early working hours put most people off going there. Flower shops generally stock up with flowers at least twice a week, and on receiving their flowers they cut and condition them before selling them as cut flowers or making them up into arrangements. Most good shops keep flowers as cool as possible and only show what is necessary out in the shop, keeping some things in a cellar or cold room out of sight. You must, however, be choosy when buying flowers and reject anything that looks as if it has been in the shop for too long or is past its best.

Street markets and flower stalls offer an inexpensive way to buy flowers. Without the overheads of premises and staff a stall should be able to offer the customer good value. Again, though, be careful when you buy and ask yourself what might be wrong with something being sold at too cheap a price. Look out for a stall that has a fast turnover and get to know the owner — that way you are less likely to be fobbed off with flowers past their prime. A stall may not offer much in the way of unusual or exotic flowers, but it should provide basic, useful stuff and certain seasonal specialities. Some days there will be bargains or a bulk buy of one particular type of flower. It is best to choose what to buy once you have got to the stall; rather like shopping for food, don't go with a firm idea of what you might buy, but rather pick the best thing available that day.

In the summer months in the country you may find bunches of seasonal flowers for sale at the roadside or cottage gate. Usually the result of a hobby, or a glut of some particular flower, consider buying them whenever you see them. The price is bound to be reasonable, and you may find wonderful flowers rarely seen for sale in shops.

FLOWERS FROM THE GARDEN

IF YOU HAVE EVEN THE SMALLEST PATCH OF GROUND to use to grow flowers then it makes good sense to plant a few specially for cutting. There are five basic categories of plants which you might choose to grow.

TREES AND SHRUBS

MANY TREES AND SHRUBS are grown to clothe and fill a garden right through the year, and annually have blossoms, leaves, fruits or berries which are very useful to the flower arranger. You might not plant shrubs specially for this purpose — though many keen flower arrangers do to get just the right coloured or variegated foliage they want — but if you are planting any new trees or shrubs or are beginning a garden from scratch, consider what might be useful to cut for the house. For example, many of the salix or willow family have wonderfully coloured stems in the winter months when colour is so scarce in the garden. Sprays of golden yellow forsythia are always a joy to bring indoors in early spring to cheer a dull room. All the viburnums have beautiful flowers and many are scented, while lilac is a must even though its

flowering is brief and its leaves dull for the rest of the year. Useful shrubs and trees which provide good foliage include mahonia, magnolia, beech, choisyia, many of the silver-leaved sun lovers such as senecio, and herbs such as rosemary and rue. Eucalyptus is renowned for its use as a filler foliage and there are many other trees which provide pretty and unusual leaves, such as maple, cotinus, and the sorbus family.

For berries to brighten autumn arrangements plant some of the rugosa roses or some of the many wild species of rose such as *Rosa myeseii*. Cotoneaster never fails to provide berries, while for a cool, white look try the snowberry (*Symphoricarpus*), not forgetting dwarf crab apples and pyracanthas.

HERBACEOUS PERENNIALS

THIS GROUP OF PLANTS can be grown in borders with others of the same type or, as is quite commonly seen these days, in a mixed border planted with shrubs, roses, bulbs and annuals. Some herbaceous perennials need a certain amount of maintenance (such as splitting and dividing some years), but they generally

Peonies (above) are magnificent flowers, though, sadly, their flowering period is very brief. Make the most of them in sumer arrangements or dry them when they are just opening out from the bud stage.

Facing page top: a perfect peony bloom.

Facing page bottom: a floribunda rose.

repay any effort, providing a backbone of colour right through the season. You may not be inclined to pick from a plant making a fine display in a border, but a few stems here and there will probably not be missed. Most perennials begin flowering in the early summer and some varieties go on until the first frosts. Some, such as Michaelmas daisies, don't get into their stride until quite late into the autumn, while a few, such as doronicum and troillus, start their flowering in late spring. A list of some perennials which would be useful to any flower arranger might include: *Alchemilla mollis*, gypsophila, hardy geranium, scabious, pinks, delphiniums, hollyhocks, peony, hemoracalis, astrantia, aquilegia, campanula, achillea, hellebore, primula and euphorbia. There are many, many more but your choice will depend to a great degree on the style and type of garden that you have.

HARDY AND HALF-HARDY ANNUALS

THIS GROUP OF FLOWERS is easy to grow and very rewarding in the amount of flowers you get from a single packet of seeds. Such bright, cheerful flowers are often scorned as being unsophisticated or even vulgar, but some of the best are as exquisite as any other flower in the plant kingdom and deserve to be included in every garden. Many hardy annuals can be sown in autumn for early summer flowering the following year, or seed can be sown in the spring after the soil has warmed up to come into bloom a little later in the summer. Many annuals thrive in sun and soil which isn't too rich as this can produce too much foliage and too few flowers, though they certainly don't like to be starved either.

When they come into bloom it pays to keep picking them regularly as they are apt to flower less once they have set seed. Some annuals, such as sweet peas and cornflowers, are a flower arranger's must, while many other varieties just aren't available unless you grow them yourself. It is sometimes easier to grow annuals in a row in a vegetable garden than to plant them in a border amongst larger, coarser plants which may smother them and take away sun and light while the annuals are developing. In a row the plants can be thinned if necessary, weeded and watered with ease and cutting for the house is made nice and simple.

Half-hardy annuals take a bit more time and effort to grow from seed, but many types are available as bedding plants later in the season if you don't have the right conditions to raise your own. Half-hardy annuals need to be sown from seed very early in the spring in gentle heat. The small plants are pricked out to grow on before being planted out after the frosts have gone. This group contains some quite exotic varieties as well as those that are simply tender in northern climates.

Here is a list of some of the many hardy annuals worth growing for flower arranging: borage, marigold, poppy in all varieties, sweet peas, dill, fennel, clarkia, godetia, nasturtium, cornflower, love-in-a-mist, larkspur, helichrysum, lavatera, sunflower, grasses of all types, helipterum, and candytuft.

Some half-hardy annuals to grow for picking include zinnia, nicotiana, eustoma, African marigolds, French marigolds, moluccella, and antirrhinums.

The next group of flowers is biennial, which means that seed is sown one year to flower the following spring or summer. There are some very pretty and useful flowers in this group, which are fine grown in a space just for cutting, or will blend happily with other types of plants. Some good examples of biennials include foxgloves, wallflowers, canterbury bells, sweet williams, forget-me-nots, honesty and stock.

BULBS, CORMS, TUBERS AND RHIZOMES

MANY FLOWERS GROWN FROM BULBS produce beautiful cut flowers — just think of lilies, daffodils and tulips. Many of them are lovely to grow in pots to force into early flowering, and if you plant a patch of narcissus, for example, think of planting a few extra to

Roses (facing page) make marvellous cut flowers, and garden grown varieties are usually tougher and more interesting than bought blooms. Home grown roses also have a beautiful fragrance if you plant the right types and they are available in a very wide range of colours.

The tall stiff stems and brilliant yellow daisy type flowers (above) of the Rudbeckia family make it a spendid garden border plant for late summer and a useful source of material for the flower arranger.

African marigolds (left) are commonly grown as bedding plants and as path borders. Their colour can be almost overpowering and their scent is not very pleasant, but they keep flowering for month after month and, wired individually, they can be air dried very successfully.

pick and bring indoors. Some good flowers in this section include daffodils, tulips, lilies, Dutch iris, alliums, hyacinths, grape hyacinths, amaryllis, camassias, anemones, ranunculus, eremurus and gladioli.

FLOWERS FOR FREE

AT ONE TIME, before we became aware of the disappearance of so many species of plants and the need for conservation, it was easy to walk along roadsides and in fields picking whatever was on offer. Nowadays, with many flowers protected and fewer and fewer to be found growing wild, it is really best to leave flowers for others to see and enjoy. There are some plants which still grow abundantly and you may be lucky enough to have wild species growing in your garden or along your verge, but if you do pick remember to be sparing and never pull a plant up roots and all. Grasses are useful for arrangements and for drying, while in the autumn there are often plenty of berries and richly coloured foliage. Moss is useful for all kinds of purposes and still very plentiful, as is lichen, if you live in an unpolluted atmosphere.

If you enjoy wild flowers and like to use them in arrangements, try growing some yourself in your garden from the many varieties of wild seed now available.

Top: the steely blue, thistle-like globes of Echinops ritro *make an imposing sight at the back of a herbaceous border. Picked before they are fully open, they are easily dried, or can be used fresh.*

Above: another thistle-type flower, eryngium or sea holly. A mass of mauvish blue flowers are produced which last and last and dry very successfully. Both plants are long-lived perennials which are easy to grow well.

*The deep purple spikes of this dwarf lavender scent the whole garden
on a still, warm summer's day. Lavender makes a perfect path edging
and attracts bees and butterflies, which feed on its nectar. It has
traditionally been used as a culinary and medicinal herb throughout
its long history. Plant a row for picking fresh and to dry for pot pourri
and lavender sachets. Its astringent yet beautiful scent is evocative of
country gardens and French Provençal fields.*

Above: bunches of lavender hung to dry. This deep purple variety holds its colour well and, of course, retains its scent.

Helichrysums (right) are crisp and dry even as they grow on the plant. Picked at just the right stage, they go on opening as they dry until the flower is perfectly open. They are often wired before hanging as the stems are too weak to support the flower head.

Santolina (above) is very pretty grown as a low hedge, and the little lemon yellow flowers dry successfully, though they are fiddly to harvest. Some people prefer to remove the flowers simply to enjoy the soft grey foliage, which can be cut and trimmed into quite strict shapes.

Above: rows of perennial chillea grown for drying. They also make a pretty cut flower, and each year new colours are developed and produced for the commercial grower.

A mixed border (left) that contains shrubs, herbaceous plants, herbs and foliage is one of the prettiest ways of gardening and provides all the year round material for the flower arranger.

Above: rich but sombre purple, abundant in the garden in late summer. Here spires of a variety of loosestrife add a magnificent splash of colour to a large border. The tall, straight spires carry flowers along their length, and are easy to grow.

Facing page: a magnificent specimen of one of the viticella varieties of clematis clambering up a wall and on into the branches of an old pear tree.

Clematis flowers (facing page) are in fact made up of bracts rather than petals, but make one of the most spectacular climbers in a garden. A few heads picked and arranged in a glass last for several days.

Above: rich pickings from the garden in a wonderful mixture of purple and blue, including hardy geraniums, astrantia, cornflowers, lavender, clematis and echium.

Statice (left) is an annual immortelle which comes in a vast colour range. It is commonly seen for sale in bunches of dried flowers, but is fun to use fresh from the garden, when its colours are very vivid and strong.

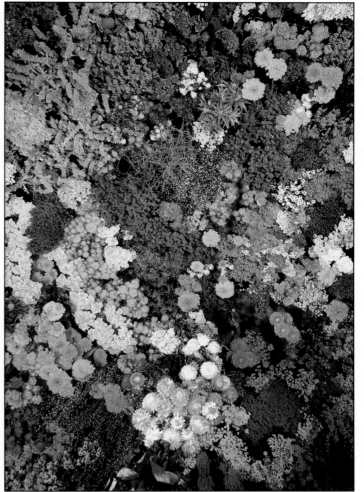

This flower stall (left) in Bond Street, London has as good a choice of flowers as many shops. With a quick turnover of stock and prices which are often reasonable, a stall is a good place to buy cut flowers for arranging at home.

Top: a roof space filled with bunches of dried flowers waiting to be used in arrangements. The mix of colours and textures is like a magnificent embroidery.

Above: the delicate flowers of the extremely vigorous climbing rose Filipes kiftsgate. This plant can climb fifty metres or more into a tree or along a wall, and fills the air around it with the most wonderful scent.

CHAPTER 4

COLOUR SCHEMING

INTRODUCTION

C OLOUR IS AN EMOTIVE and difficult subject to deal with as the experience of colour is a very personal and subjective thing. Individual people appear to see colours in different ways, and we all have special preferences and hates, based on goodness knows what, which persist throughout our lives. Perhaps a lot of the problems to do with colour lie in the language difficulties involved in trying to describe something so intangible. One person's mauve is another's pink, while whether we describe a blue as turquoise or green may depend on what our parents taught us, never checking back to the colour of a real piece of turquoise or, in the case of pink, back to peach

Colour stirs up very strong emotions and it is a proven fact that rooms of different colours can affect the way we feel or think at a particular, time and even make us feel happy or depressed, warm or cold. Flowers must carry one of the greatest ranges of colour in nature and, though we get so used to seeing them, a special, brilliant red poppy or a true blue gentian still has the power to stop someone in their tracks as if seen for the first time. Pure colour reaches us very directly and perhaps never more so than through the petals of a flower.

There are really no hard and fast rules when it comes to using colours of flowers. There are a few guidelines and one or two facts

Sometimes the most daring colour combinations (facing page) are the most successful. This mix of very hot colours looks wonderful in a plain glass tank. The flowers include poppies, schizanthus, honeysuckle, double buttercups and thrift.

Above: a cool and fresh scheme using white freesias, yellow alstroemeria, roses and pale blue delphiniums. The yellow fruit accentuates the sunniness of this kitchen arrangement.

The strong yellow colour of the gerbera (above) is a deeper tone of the wall behind them and the yellow flowers in the fabric.

Left: Shirley poppies silhouetted in a window. The colour range of these flowers is dramatic and beautiful. Fleeting they may be, but their short life is full of colour and drama. Poppy seeds should be sown in every garden as they are so easy to grow.

worth knowing, but more often than not you need to let your eye do the work and your senses the rest. In nature the colour scheming is invariably right. The pale lemon and gold of a wild daffodil is perfectly offset by the blue green of a daffodil leaf. Things only start to go wrong when we change and hybridise plants, making them bigger and brighter at the expense of subtlety and form.

Some people believe orange and pink clash, while others say that in nature nothing clashes — points like these will depend on what you have learnt over the years. The important thing is always to be open-minded and prepared to experiment. Until you actually put one coloured flower with another or try an orange marigold in a purple vase you will never get a clear view. If you feel shy about using bold, strong colours then cultivate subtlety and softness and learn to mix clear pastels or chalky, pale tones. A good trick to remember when arranging flowers if you are muddled about the colours you have put together is to half-close your eyes. This distances you from what you are looking at and knocks out the form but enhances the tones, almost as if you were working in black and white, which often helps you to see more clearly and work out what to do next.

COLOUR SCHEMING

COLOURS FALL INTO TWO DISTINCT RANGES, the primary colours and the secondary colours. The primaries are pure red, yellow and blue, which exist as themselves and cannot be made from any other colours. The secondary colours are made from mixing two primary colours together in various proportions, such as blue and yellow to create green, yellow and red to make orange and red and blue to make purple.

By adding white to pure colours you produce tints, such as pink and cream, while adding black to a pure colour results in a shade. In nature the range of colours is never-ending, and many plants will even hold dozens of variations of one colour.

Colours definitely have a character of which you need to be aware. Red, for example, is strong and warm and tends to come towards you, while blue recedes like a clear summer sky or the coolness of miles of ocean. Green is fresh and restful, yellow warm again, the colour of sunshine and life. Purple can be either sombre or rich and orange is always brash and full of fire. If you make a wheel of the six primary and secondary colours you will find which are the complementary or opposite colours. Red is opposite green, blue is opposite orange and yellow to purple.

Colours from the same side of the wheel will always harmonise safely but, as a spark of contrast is often necessary to bring an arrangement to life, so it is important to know a little about the physics of colour.

This dramatic bedroom setting needed equally exciting flowers. A winter mixture of dyed eucalyptus leaves, silver artificial leaves and fresh cotoneaster branches emphasises the blue already in the room's colour scheme, while subtly bringing out the green.

PLANNING A COLOUR SCHEME

YOUR STARTING POINT for planning a flower arrangement colour scheme may well be the colour of the room in which the flowers are going to stand. This could lead you on to choosing flowers in similar colours but perhaps using a darker or lighter version so that they stand out from the furnishings and don't merge into the background. You may choose a colour very similar to the surroundings but decide to add an accent of a different, sharper colour, or simply provide plenty of green to off-set the flowers. You might choose a much stronger statement by picking a completely contrasting colour for flower and furnishings, or else you may play safe with a cool and elegant arrangement in shades of cream or white. This choice is ideal, but of course there are many times when a colour scheme can't be planned, perhaps because you have just been given some flowers, or you have picked what there is in the garden or grabbed a bunch of whatever is left at the supermarket. Don't worry, it is very rare that a flower arrangement looks completely wrong because the colours haven't been chosen more carefully.

HARMONY OR CONTRAST?

SOME OF THE MOST SUCCESSFUL flower arrangements are those using several closely related colours; for example, a mix of mauves, pale blues and pinks. This combination is soft and restful and always pretty, as would be an arrangement made from flowers in pale yellows and creams. In both cases a good measure of green is necessary to define the different colours and to bring a little relief into what could become rather monotonous.

In a totally different spirit the use of contrasting colours can produce something very strong and definitely not subtle. Mixing flowers in, say, bright lemon yellow and mid blue could look stunning — or it could look disastrous. It would be important to use a sympathetic container perhaps in clear glass, plain white china or a faded old blue and white design. Again this mixture would need the relief of some fresh green in it and even the addition of some white flowers, ideally white daisies with yellow centres, which would tie the whole thing together. Red and green are contrasting colours that work well in arrangements. This colour scheme has become a cliché at Christmas when it appears in many versions and always looks festive, rich and traditional. Mixing many different hot reds and pinks plus a little orange can look exotic, stunning and very dramatic — a wonderful colour scheme in the autumn when nature successfully combines these colours with ease. Try an arrangement of glossy red and orange berries, shocking pink nerines, rich red and orange chrysanthemums and brilliant pink, orange and red leaves which have turned colour after a frost. You can probably do without green in this version as the foliage will have in it a certain number of bronze shades and subtle colours to tone down the warmth of the flower colours.

Facing page: the warmth of rich apricot roses and spray carnations contrasts with the acid lime green of euphorbia and guelder rose blossoms. To cool the arrangement down, plenty of white has been added using thick sprays of lilac.

Left: palest apricot and mauvish blue, one of the softest and prettiest colour combinations. Green is added in the form of young, brilliant grass-green beech leaves, and the whole arrangement softened with loose, white sprays of Queen Anne's Lace.

Above left: deep, warm tones of orange with a hint of green in an autumn chrysanthemum and bare twig arrangement.

Above: blue and pale light green look cool and attractive together. The deep blue of the hyacinth blooms is mixed with Hellebore foetidus and Hellebore niger plus the white-traced foliage of Arum italicum.

A white and green colour scheme is one of the most sophisticated you
can choose. Here, the highly scented flowers of Lilium longiflorum
are used with eucalyptus foliage and stems of papyrus.

*Autumn sees a change in the colours of garden flowers and plants.
Vine leaves (above left) take on red tints and there are clusters of
berries to use, as well as rich red sedum flowers.*

*High summer provides brilliant pinks, crimsons and cerises (above
right). Honeysuckle, foxgloves, Rosa officinalis, clematis and
pelargoniums will all need some cool green added to calm their colour
down and to add definition and contrast.*

COLOUR THEMES

THERE ARE MANY TRIED AND TESTED colour combinations which are well worth copying and which don't rely on any particular flowers to produce the right results.

Pale apricot and soft sky blue look lovely together with just a little very fresh acidic green such as you find in young beech leaves of *Helleborus foetidissima*. Plenty of green, with just a little of both yellow and white, has the very essence of spring about it. The yellow can be sharp and citrus or rich and golden.

Apricot and peachy pinks work well together, ranging through from the palest blush shell pink to rich coral. Off-set what could be a rather cloying effect with fresh greens or a soft blue-green or grey. Silver and white is always stunning, as could be pure white with cream and green variegated foliage or plain green leaves. The foliage is essential with white flowers as these need a solid background for their shapes to register. The only time this would not be necessary is when the white flowers stand in silhouette against a very dark background. White flowers have an inbuilt sophistication and elegance, and light up a dark room like nothing else. If you are ever puzzled over what to choose for a colour scheme then you can't go wrong with an all white arrangement. The simple, sculptural shapes of white lilies look timeless, while a jar of fluffy, white daisies, though completely artless and unsophisticated, still has an eye-catching effect. Understatement is often harder to achieve then a dazzling effect, but if you choose white then you are half-way there.

Orange flowers are often hard to place in an interior. The brashness of this colour (which always screams out to be noticed) needs a subtle toning down with browns or dull greens. Natural autumn oranges are often more subtle as the colour has gone through an ageing or fading process and is softer and more gentle. Beware really fierce orange on its own — though, surprisingly, this can sometimes look magnificent used with many other equally powerful colours such as crimson, purple, royal blue and strong yellow.

This mixing of many different colours can look spectacular in the way that an eighteenth-century flower still-life painting does. So that no particular colour jumps out from the overall composition it is important to keep all the tones of equal strength throughout the arrangement. If any colours do dominate, then group them together and surround them with colours likely to soften the effect. Spreading them through the arrangement simply results in a very jumpy, spotty look.

The seasons seem to suggest a pattern of colour variations running from winter whites and creams to golden spring yellows and greens, with a dash of purple and mauve, then moving on to summer colours of pinks, mauves and blues and late summer crimsons, deep reds and purples and into autumn tints ranging from harvest yellows and oranges and vivid scarlets and pinks. Finally there are the rich, deep browns of nuts and dying leaves and glossy evergreen leaves with the odd accent of winter berries. If you don't know where to begin, look around and take a cue from the seasons.

CHAPTER 5

PUTTING IT ALL TOGETHER

INTRODUCTION

 LOWER CHOICES and the way we put arrangements together have changed over the centuries, though not as much as houses or lifestyles. Flowers and plants are really just as they have always been, and even the containers that we use nowadays are similar to those used in Roman times or in the sixteenth or eighteenth centuries. We can probably presume that for as long as there has been some kind of vessel to put flowers in and prolong their life away from the plant, people have been decorating their homes with flowers.

In some countries flowers are of spiritual and religious meaning; particular flowers are used for special occasions and arranged in special ways. We see flowers nowadays as a very important ingredient to all kinds of social functions as well as simply a means of decorating and adding colour to a house. As there are professionals who work at putting together arrangements and displays, many ordinary people are scared to have a go themselves. This a shame, as anyone with the dexterity to handle a pair of scissors and fill a container with water can make a stunning display with a few decent flowers. Certain myths and ideas have sprung up about the right and wrong way to arrange flowers and, constrained by these, many people miss out on great enjoyment and satisfaction.

Flower clubs and classes often tend to give people the impression that there are standards to attain and rules of prop-

Flowers which have a lot of foliage along the stems should be stripped clean (facing page). Some leaves can be left near the flower heads, but any lower foliage which might be under water in the vase must be removed, or it will rot and turn the water cloudy and unpleasant.

Woody stems of shrubs and trees should be split or hammered on the lower section of the stem (above). This will help the plant to absorb water once it is in a vase and prolong the time it stays fresh. The stem should be cut at an angle to allow the maximum absorbent surface area to be in contact with the water.

Some flowers, such as alstroemeria (top), benefit from having their foliage cut away completely. The flowers are long-lived but the greenery soon looks tired and tends to hide the blooms. This is very much a matter of personal taste and will, of course, depend on the type of arrangement you require.

Lilies (above) have beautiful stamens which are smothered with deep orange pollen. If the pollen falls on clothing or furnishings it can stain permanently. If brushed off lightly when dry the mark is not too bad, but when mixed with water the pollen stains a dark orange. If there is a danger of this happening, cut off all the stamens.

ortion and balance to which they must adhere. These restraints are simply the framework necessary for teaching something to someone else. The teacher who simply says 'do what you like' and 'just get on with it' is likely to confuse someone wanting to learn, so rules are invented for people to follow and know where they are. The problem with this approach is that it's likely to stifle spontaneity, encouraging instead a kind of painting-by-numbers mentality that produces contrived and rather static groups of flowers which never look right except in a formal interior or on a show bench. You must be prepared to relax and experiment a bit, trying out all kinds of mixtures and styles. There are no right and wrong ways to do things, only the way you like things to look. Throughout the book there are hundreds of very different arrangements of flowers to inspire you, and in this chapter there are some guidelines and ideas for achieving a happy result.

CUTTING AND PREPARING

IF YOU PICK FLOWERS from a garden yourself then you will have the chance to cut blooms which are at their best. The ideal times of day to pick plant material are early in the morning and in the evening, as at both these times the flowers' cells are full of moisture. During the middle of the day the air temperature is usually warmer and the plant will have lost moisture to the atmosphere.

Cut stems cleanly on a slant with a very sharp pair of secateurs, scissors or a knife, and stand them in a bucket of water in a cool place for at least a few hours. Very cold water will cause shock to the plant, so aim for a temperature of around 21°C (70°F). The ideal arrangement is to pick during the evening, leaving flowers overnight for use the next morning.

If you buy flowers they will probably have been conditioned in this way in the shop, but it is a good idea to re-cut the stems at a slant and stand them in a bucket of water for at least a couple of hours before arranging them. Certain flowers and plants need special treatment to make them last as long as possible. Poppies, poinsettias and members of the euphorbia family should have the ends of their stems seared over a flame. Dahlias, ferns and hellebore species need to have their stems dipped in boiling water for up to forty seconds before being given a soak. Large, hollow stems, such as those on delphiniums and lupins, can be filled with water and then plugged with a small piece of cotton wool. This holds the moisture in but allows the plant to continue drinking water from the container. Tulips can be perverse and difficult. Once arranged the stems often twist and carry on growing into wonderful curving shapes. This can look lovely or it can be a nuisance. Wrapping the bunch of tulips tightly in paper before conditioning keeps them in good shape. Other spring bulb flowers should always be trimmed beyond the white part of the stem into the green to help their water absorption, and these need a soak on their own before arranging. The sap from flowers such as daffodils can affect others in a mixed arrangement.

Except very furry or silver leaves, most types of foliage benefit from a period of complete immersion in water before use. You will need a very large sink or something of equivalent size to do this. All tough and woody stems of foliage or flowers must be thoroughly split or crushed to allow water to travel up them. Do

Well prepared and conditioned flowers will last a long time, so it is
not worth skimping this stage if you have spent a lot of time and
money on a large, elaborate arrangement. As flowers fade or die,
remove them and either add a few more or let the whole thing gently
fade. Never leave dead blooms inamongst fresh ones as this will ruin
the whole effect.

All flowers benefit from a long drink (*above*) before they are
arranged. If you buy flowers from a shop they will probably have
been given this treatment, and the foliage and thorns may well have
been removed.

Roses have been bred which are almost thornless (*facing page*), but
you will probably still need to do a bit of cleaning up along the stems.
Remove leaves and thorns by scraping with the edge of a scissor blade
or a special tool.

this by hammering the bottom few centimetres, or else cut up along the stem with a knife or secateurs. Give woody stemmed flowers a long drink before arranging them. Roses should have their thorns and small leaves removed before use, the stems should be crushed or split and all stems that will be submerged below the water level should be cleaned of leaves or branches which otherwise will rot and cloud the water.

RECONDITIONING AND AFTER CARE

AN ARRANGEMENT using floral foam will need to be topped up regularly with water as long as the flowers last. Once the foam has dried out it is very difficult to get it to re-absorb more moisture. Containers which have just water in them should have the water changed if it no longer looks fresh, or topped up as required. There are special preservatives available which, dissolved into the water, are designed to prolong the life of the flowers and keep the water sweet. If you have used some of this product then simply top up with water if necessary but don't change it completely. If after a little time flowers suddenly droop or look rather sad it is some-times possible to revive them with drastic action. Take the flowers out of the vase and cut all the ends of the stems by about two centimetres. Stand the flowers in hot shallow water for approx-imately ten minutes. Remove them and then leave them in deep, cool water for another hour or so before re-arranging them. This treatment often brings quite hopeless cases back to life.

Some people swear by other additives to keep flowers lasting as long as possible, such as aspirin, a spoonful of white sugar or carbonated drinks.

PROPORTION AND SIZE

CHOOSING THE RIGHT SHAPE and size of container to suit certain flowers is probably one area of flower arranging which causes people the most problems. There are no hard and fast rules to adhere to but there are a few basic guidelines. Visually, a container should have the right weight for the flowers it holds; in other words a thin, spindly vase with a chunky mass of flowers at the top will look awkward and unbalanced — as well as probably falling over in reality —, while a small and squat container will look strange with very long-stemmed flowers inside it. Very generally, the flowers should be up to two thirds of the overall height of flowers and container. Any bigger proportion of flowers to vase may give a top-heavy look. In reverse, a very large and dramatic container will look peculiar with a small arrangement in it or only a few blooms perched in the top. These simple decisions about scale are usually quite easy to make, and as you become more experienced you will find they become automatic.

Before you begin an arrangement leave stems as long as possible and cut them to size as you work. For arrangements where the flowers are densely packed near the top of the container, cut all stems to the same length, measuring where to cut them by holding the flowers against the vase and deciding on the height you want. If you have just a few flowers of the same kind to make into some sort of arrangement they will invariably look best cut fairly short and packed into a small container. This will give the illusion of mass and generosity, when spreading a few stems out in a large container can't look thin and mean. Don't be frightened

to cut down long stems to just a centimetre or two if you wish. Just because a flower comes with a long stem there is no need to keep it that way. Growers produce many types of flowers with as long a stem as possible to give the arranger a choice of uses, but never feel that you can't be in control of the material that you have. For example, a gladioli flower cut down or split into individual flowers takes on a new character and can be used in a way totally different from those with a long stiff stem.

STYLE AND SHAPE

BEFORE YOU PUT FLOWERS into an arrangement you will need to consider where the finished display is going to be, how high or low it will be, where it will be lit from, and whether it will be seen from all round, above, or only from one side. If you can, work at the same height as the flowers will eventually be so that you get the right eye level for the arrangement. Flowers standing in a window or with the main light source from behind them loose colour and definition, but the outline will be a silhouette and therefore important to consider. An arrangement for a low table looks best if it is symmetrical and can be viewed from all round, while the view from above is obviously important too. Arrangements standing on high shelves or pieces of furniture are best put into low containers to avoid a top-heavy look; given a wider base than height add a few trails of foliage onto the surface to suggest a lower centre of gravity and keep the flowers from appearing to float.

Think about backgrounds to an arrangement and how they can enhance the look of your flowers. A very busily patterned fabric or wallpaper needs simple, crisp outlines and solid shapes. Plain backgrounds and flat colours will throw delicate tracery and fine details into relief. Make use of what you have in the way of surroundings to make more of your flowers. Group more than one container of flowers to make a greater impact, maybe making your

Tulips (right) can be tricky flowers with wills of their own. Once in water they often bend and grow towards a light source. This looks pretty and relaxed, but if you want them upright, wrap them tightly in a bunch with newspaper and stand them in deep water overnight.

Below: the simplest and most effective way of treating tulips. Retaining most of the tulips' foliage, if it is in good shape, looks informal and gives the impression of flowers that have come straight from the garden. A plain, glass, fish-bowl-shaped vase is the perfect container for this effect.

Tulips make good mixers, and work well with many other spring flowers such as pink ranunculus, rose buds and just a few tulip leaves.

flower arrangement part of a collection of different objects like a still life or tablescape. Mix other elements with flowers to contrast or bring out the colours and textures of both materials. Try adding fruits or pebbles, objects such as small pieces of wood, an exquisite feather, a collection of shells or simply bits and pieces that you like. Use seasonal produce to inspire a flower idea such as a large, golden pumpkin or a big bunch of brilliant green parsley.

If you simply don't know how to start an arrangement make the easiest possible version — a posy or bunch. To do this, the flowers and foliage need to be roughly the same length and all you do is to hold a stem or two in one hand and add to it moving the bunch round and loosening it as you go until you have a handful which is fairly open and evenly spaced. Tie or wire it if you like and trim the ends to the length you need to fit it all into a container. A jug or simple, wide-necked vase would be ideal. This is an almost foolproof way to get a pretty result, and a bunch made like this makes a perfect gift.

Faced with a mass of very different flowers and foliage the first thing to do is to sort out the material that you have into groups so that you can see quite clearly how much there is and exactly what it is. Group types and colours of flowers together, then lay the colour groups beside each other to see what looks best against what and whether there are any which are quite wrong and need to be discarded. Seeing plant material in this way helps you to work out a balance of colour and shape before you begin. For a dense and textural type of arrangement it is often best to keep the flowers in small bunches or groups rather than using them individually, but if you prefer to work one flower at a time then do.

MAKING A START

MANY PEOPLE BEGIN with a framework of foliage or filling material to set the outline and limits of an arrangement before filling in with the important flowers. Rather like drawing a picture before painting, this is a very useful way to build up an arrangement. You could also start by using the large and important flowers or plant material which you want to have pride of place and working round them. The former method is most commonly used but it's really your choice as to how you want to work.

SECTION 2

Arrangements for the House

CHAPTER 1

ROOM BY ROOM

VERY ROOM IN THE HOUSE will benefit from having flowers in it. A room without something fresh and alive in it never feels as lived in or cared for as one with even the simplest bunch of colourful blooms or a plant or two in the window. We can fill rooms with floral prints and fabrics to echo the summer garden borders we love, but a vase of real garden blooms brings the outside inside. Apart from their wonderful colours and textures, flowers also often add fragrance to a room — no spray fresheners and artificial scents can ever match the real thing.

You might choose to put very different flowers in each setting in a house or else choose a style you like which looks fine throughout. It will depend on the space and the type of furnishings you have. A hall, if it has the space, can take quite large and formal arrangements. It is always pleasant to be greeted by flowers on opening the door, though, as some houses have quite dark halls, it may be sensible to use dried or artificial flowers in place of fresh ones. Living rooms are perfect places for flowers, usually having enough surfaces and pieces of furniture to stand them on. In the summer, fireplaces and grates look good filled with flowers and in the winter months, when the room is used often with artificial lighting, small arrangements spotlighted or standing in a pool of light beneath a table lamp look warm and rich. Low coffee tables are the ideal place to stand shallow baskets

Facing page: an exhuberant
mixture of deep pink
antirrhinums, lilies, hydrangea
heads and euphorbia. Arranged
on an occasional table, the
whole thing could be moved
around to find the
perfect position.

Above: pink stargazer lilies
mixed with pale blue brodiaea,
spray carnations and euphorbia
arranged in a shallow, pink
Wedgwood fruit dish.

Right: sprays of apple blossom
from the garden are used with
rich, pinky-red spray carnations
and sprays of delicate
London pride.

A dramatic background demands rich and sumptuous flowers. Above: pale spikes of cream stocks, honeysuckle, alstroemeria and roses mixed with garden foliage and Queen Anne's lace from the hedgerow. The use of unusual foliage gives a rich, old-fashioned country house feel.

At the end of winter the first daffodils are a great pleasure. They are used here with red tulips, white chrysanthemums and plenty of glossy, dark green evergreen foliage (left).

Facing page: an unexpected use of colour in a spectacular setting. The use of arching stems adds greatly to the impact of the arrangement. Mauvy-blue hydrangeas are mixed with red lilies and golden yellow euphorbia sprays.

filled with groups of small flowering plants such as miniature cyclamen or primulas, or tightly packed bunches of 'solid' flowers such as anemones or ranunculus.

Kitchens are for working in, so flowers must never impede or clutter the space there, but a simple arrangement can do a lot to cheer a sleek and modern fitted kitchen or add a homely touch to a country-style kitchen based around warm, natural materials. A jug or mug of flowers on the kitchen table is always welcome, while herbs or pots of growing flowers work well on a kitchen windowsill.

Bedrooms sometimes get neglected when it comes to flowers, but these can look lovely here with a little thought as these rooms are often pretty and feminine. The Victorians believed that flowers were unhealthy in a bedroom and removed them at night. This fear seems to have lingered, and people often never think to make pretty bedside posies or put a single, beautiful rose bloom beside a dressing table mirror. Small touches such as these can give great pleasure, especially in a guest room. A bathroom too can benefit from the flower treatment or, at the very least, a flowering plant that will thrive in the warm, humid atmosphere.

Right: a soft and very pleasing effect achieved with stems of tiny white Michaelmas daisies, appearing like stars from a firework. Delphiniums, veronica and celosia make solid shapes which give the arrangement its stability.

Below: vivid, velvety anemones look warm and inviting standing amongst a blue and white china collection. Anemones are useful flowers for winter arrangements.

A pair of arrangements gives perfect symmetry to a formal setting.
The intense blue delphiniums are used with deep red carnations and
pure white irises. Plenty of greenery keeps the colour scheme fresh.

Putting flowers in a hall is traditional and pleasing. They welcome visitors and set the tone for the whole house. Left: an autumnal arrangement that fills the whole mahogany table with sprays of wild clematis, fuchsia, warm, orangey lilies, protea, arching deep orange euphorbia and red roses. The great variety of leaves used is what makes this arrangement so special, and it is a good example of using seasonal materials at their best.

A room which is busy with pattern in the furnishings needs cool and sophisticated flowers. Top: simple liles provide shape, and red roses are added to echo the floral fabric.

Above: a predominantly cream arrangement for the corner of a landing. The arrangement is in a quite loose, informal style and makes wonderful use of many different types of foliage and berries, providing a foil for white and pale pink lilies, cream carnations and hydrangeas.

Above: a delicious spring basketful of pink hyacinths and ranunculus with pale lemon freesias and narcissi.

Above right: a sculptural and dramatic arrangement made from protea and stems of celosia or cockscomb.

Kitchens demand plain and simple arrangements like these small posies of peach gerbera and frothy white gypsophila (right).

A summer fireplace can look empty and unattractive, so it is a perfect place to stand a large, colourful arrangement. Below left: many colours put together using purple iris, yellow lilies, forsythia, genista, tulips and gerbera.

Below: a winter decoration when flowers are scarce. A few scented white freesia are put with variegated ivies, euonymus and sprigs of yew, and, for a festive feel, a few sprigs of mistletoe are added, with gilded grapes as the finishing touch.

A modern setting needs uncompromisingly simple flowers. This
stunning arrangement becomes the focal point of the whole room.
The strong colour scheme has been carried through from the fabrics to
the flowers. Imposing yellow arum lilies have been added to a simple
structure of bare twigs and yellow genista, and this whole
arrangement has been placed in a water-filled bowl together with
floating petals. The reflective surface below makes the flowers
appear to float.

A sumptuous bedroom needs little extra decoration, but a shallow bowl of exquisite, velvety roses at the bedside adds another touch of fin-de-siècle opulence (left).

Fresh, cheerful Iceland poppies (top) look best arranged on their own. Their papery texture and brilliant range of colours looks quite at home in a kitchen setting.

A bathroom isn't always the most practical room in which to display flowers, but there are occasions, say when guests are expected, when it is good to make a special effort. Keep arrangements small and stable, such as this fresh spring bowl of hyacinth, narcissi, ranunculus and genista (above).

It is pleasant sometimes to use flowers in a very simple way to see them uncluttered and in a different light. Above: stems of sweetly scented pink lilies make strong and beautiful shapes in silhouette and have a sleek modern feel in an off-white colour scheme.

Asters (left) are old-fashioned summer flowers with not a lot of sophistication but plenty of colour and character. They look superb made into a bunch and displayed in a robust blue and white jug. In this kind of arrangement the main concern is colour and texture as the form will look after itself.

Above: an arrangement with a distinctly old-fashioned feel, using
ranunculus, sweet peas, anemones, euphorbia and larkspur.

When garden roses are in season, simply enjoy them as they are and
pick bunches to arrange loosely in a shallow bowl (below left).

Below right: a soft green jug sets off deep coral roses and sprays of
scented honeysuckle perfectly.

Above: a winter arrangement to brighten an awkward space high up on a tall piece of furniture. The shape is wide and spreading to fill the gap between ceiling and tallboy. Gold and green variegated foliage is mixed with yellow lilies and winter jasmine.

Above right: soft pinks and yellows put together with white to make a fresh and pretty spring arrangement. Sprays of lilac mingle with pink genista, ranunculus and hippeastrum with the sharp accent of lemon daffodils.

A dark position demands clear outlines and strong colour. Right: pale lilac iris combined with deep yellow tulips and daffodils with just a few carefully chosen pieces of yew and hellebore foliage.

The freshest mixture of yellows and greens results in a spectacular
arrangement to compete with the colour outside. Tne golden yellow
globes of Buddleia globosa and the creamy white tulips are balanced
by soft sprays of paler yellow solidago and the use of plenty of fresh,
green, clean-cut foliage. The arrangement has been made using a
large block of floral foam so that no container is neccessary. The
hanging arrangements are made in the same way, using a foam base
fixed to the pillar.

Top: the simplicity of tulips used on their own in a kitchen jug.

Above: a dense mass of colour and texture made using orange lilies, alstroemeria, roses, spray carnations and chrysanthemums with a few branches of rose hips to add spice.

A low, spreading arrangement will be seen from above, so it is important to make it full of interest throughout. Burnt orange gerbera and speckled lilies are the eye-catching part of the arrangement (right) and long, arching sprays of euphorbia and bare, shiny twigs reinforce the horizontal feel. Foral foam has been used to make the base.

Right: a beautiful antique workbox makes a perfect pedestal for an elegant and ambitious arrangement. The wide range of flowers used includes white lilac, freesias, hyacinths, chrysanthemums, ranunculus, gerbera and prunus.

Below: a pretty, countrified mixture arranged into a handled basket. The varied garden foliage and shrubs need only a few flowers to bring the whole thing to life. The arrangement includes hellebores, hyacinths, grape hyacinths, winter viburnum and ranunculus, with cotoneaster leaves, arum, bergenia, euphorbia and euonymus.

Above: a wonderful spring mixture of blossom, twigs and flowers showing how successfully very varied materials can be used together.

Left: a beautiful blue and white china footbath becomes the starting point for an exhuberant arrangement using a vast palette of colours. Red parrot tulips and hippeastrums are used with orange lilies, yellow gerbera and purple iris. Forsythia, Cornus mas, twisted hazel, dainty double prunus and white lilac make marvellous fillers.

*Take a lead from the colour scheme in a room to help choose flowers
which fit. The warm terracotta background here blends perfectly with
the strong, sunny yellow forsythia and scarlet tulips and lilies. A few
white and yellow irises add highlights and the strong black, classic
Wedgwood vase provides a solid contrast beneath the flowers.*

Autumn is the time to make the most of fruits and berries in arrangements and to work with all the rich foliage tints which are only available at this time of year. Right: a burnt orange 'Thirties vase makes a superb container for a rich mixture of rose hips, crab apples, cotoneaster berries and brilliant scarlet pelargonium flowers.

Below: a marvellously theatrical set piece to celebrate autumn. Bronze oak leaves and shiny gourds spill from terracotta garden pots, and a sheaf of golden yellow ornamental chillies adds drama. Above the hearth hang boughs of wild hops laden with soft green flowers. Left to dry, these will remain decorative through the winter.

Above: a summer hearth filled with chrysanthemums and carnations in soft, feminine colours, perfectly in tune with the mood of this room.

A beautiful, classical, curved niche in a drawing room (left) has been decorated in a quite formal way with a basis of deep yellow solidago and evergreen foilage studded throughout with coral pink gerbera daisies. The small trails of dark green ivy give movement to the arrangement, and soften the overall effect.

The classic furnishings (right) in this drawing room are made even more stylish by the juxtaposition of a modern and startling arrangement made using crimson trails of furry amaranthus and a bromeliad variety mixed with eucalyptus and exotic foliage.

Below: a delightfully simple arrangement for a narrow mantle shelf made from a mixture of garden and florist's flowers. Scarlet dahlias and deep coral red roses are offset by the tiny discs of santolina flowers in a fresh citrus yellow and the soft green foliage of ballota and senecio.

Top: a stunningly spectacular use of white delphinium spires, blue larkspur and peachy pink gladioli with a mass of refreshing greenery. Above: a restrained colour scheme of old rose pink and rich cream roses mixed with eucalyptus foliage for a pretty table arrangement for a dinner a deux.

The dark polished wooden furniture in a country cottage lends itself as a background to strong rich colours such as those of orange marigolds and rust coloured hemoracalis (right).

*A delicate yellow and white decoration echoes the marble
fireplace beneath it.*

Above left: rich yellow chrysanthemums and rust alstroemeria.

Above right: spring sunshine from ranunculus and genista.

Above: deep red chrysanthemums with a lime green eye.

Right: woven, nest-shaped baskets entwined with hops hold fresh fruit for a harvest celebration.

Above: rich red foliage tones with strong autumn flower colours.

Facing page top: a delightfully asymmetrical arrangement with a slightly Oriental influence in which white and yellow and pale mauve irises are mixed with yellow tulips.

Facing page bottom left: a summer garden arrangement, its inspiration taken from the vase, blends together roses, lilies, convolvulus tricolour, yellow jasmine and frothy Alchemilla mollis.

Facing page bottom right: a miniature pot of sparkling fresh snowdrops.

Above: a dramatic colour scheme for a dining room arrangement includes branches of glossy berried hypericum, red roses, apricot chrysanthemums and red spray carnations.

Left: *a pair of informal, pretty country baskets brimming with fresh, new chestnut foliage, cow parsley, anemones, hydrangeas, roses and alstroemeria. A pair of flower arrangements has enormous impact, and here works wonderfully well with the symmetry of the setting.*

Top: *a welcoming arrangement for a hall table contains generous branches of white lilac mixed with soft pink genista and brilliant orangey-red, fringed parrot tulips.*

Above: *twining garlands of smilax decorate a staircase for a special occasion, and the newel posts are transformed too, with pink lilies, bouvardia, scabious and white anthuriums.*

A conservatory extension (above) is full of sunlight, and in it a fresh colour scheme of yellow, white and green looks natural and pretty. Sprays of yellow genista are put with long-stemmed antirrhinum, narcissi and white gerbera daisies for an elegant pedestal arrangement.

Right: pure gold in a forest-green jug. Ornamental chillies are mixed with helichrysums, single chrysanthemums, alstroemeria and yellow roses. The gourds below add shape and continue the colour scheme.

Facing page top left: a basket full of soft fern, white foxgloves, roses and Alchemilla mollis.

Facing page top right: gently arching stems make a refined desk top arrangement.

Facing page bottom: the crisp black and white floor and white paintwork of this conservatory demand an unfussy arrangement. Cool white freesias are put with neat cotoneaster foliage and berries, and highlights are added in the form of long-stemmed red roses.

CHAPTER 2

MEMORABLE MEALTIMES

FOOD AND FLOWERS seem to combine well. A buffet table spread with the most delicious food will look even better with the addition of bowls of flowers. Even the simplest meal at home becomes more special when the table has some flowers on it because it suggests that the person who provides the meal and the flowers really cares that it should be enjoyed.

Dinner parties and more formal meals are a chance to dress up the table and to bring out the best china, silver and glass. Flowers can set the style or mood of the meal, though they should never be so dominant or impressive that they obscure everything else. At very grand, formal banquets where tables run the length of a room, flower arrangements, often tall and magnificent, run the length of the table, quite spoiling the chances of communication between people on either side. In a smaller setting always keep flowers low and spreading or, if you make tall arrangements, see that they are very light and delicate, consisting perhaps of just a few flowers round a candlestick. Another very pretty and effective decoration for a dinner party setting is to make tiny, individual arrangements for each guest. These could be put into small liqueur glasses or tiny coffee cups and stood in front or to the side of each place setting. The same small arrangements could also stand in a ring in the centre of a round table or be placed in a line along a rectangular one.

A single flower head makes a beautiful decoration for crisp, folded napkins at each place and can be a gift for each diner too.

A strawberry tea for two in the garden (facing page) simply needs a glass bowl of old fashioned garden roses and the frothy acid green of Alchemilla mollis to turn the meal into a special occasion.

Above: a Mediterranean breakfast of brioche, croissant and orange juice is made even sunnier by the addition of a posy of marigolds and nasturtiums.

An individual arrangement beside a place setting (left) is charming and shows thought for a guest. It can be as quick and simple as a few stems of fragrant freesias in a glass tumbler.

Buffet tables demand more impressive displays; these should be stood towards the back of a table to leave plenty of space to reach the food. The type of food presentation should be reflected in the flowers: a stylish wedding finger buffet on white linen needs elegant flowers — displayed in silver perhaps — , while a cheerful, rustic supper set out in a barn, or outdoors, demands big jugs or earthenware bowls of bright and simple country flowers. Festive occasions such as Christmas are a chance to go way over the top with wonderful still-life arrangements of flowers and fruit. Pile pyramids of fruit on platters or stemmed dishes and tuck flowers amongst them. The fruit can become part of the dessert.

Don't forget to decorate a tray with flowers for a meal in bed or for an invalid. It is never much fun eating alone, but a little bouquet of flowers works wonders for a sick person's morale.

A tiny bowl of flowers on a meal tray (facing page top) is a lovely detail and is sure to please the diner. Here soft green, dried hydrangeas are mixed with vivid yellow helichrysums.

Facing page bottom: a fresh, scented bouquet for a breakfast tray. Love-in-a-mist, veronica and pink spray carnations in a tiny container still leave room for the actual food.

Above: bright and cheerful flowers echo the flowery tray they stand on. A few stems cut short can be arranged in a tiny soufflé dish or even an egg cup

Left: very carefully chosen flowers for a supper tray include tiny dried poppy seed heads, a few euonymous berries, polygonum spikes and alstroemeria.

Top: an outdoor bouquet to complement an al fresco meal. Buttercups and daisies look sweet in a pale wicker basket.

Above centre: a few flower heads simply scattered over a dish of crisp sweet peppers creates a colourful table decoration.

Above: take your cue for colours from a tablecloth and emphasise the scheme with fruit or vegetables.

Right: a short-lived but beautifully decorative idea for a table centrepiece. Take a colourful, frilly cabbage and place small flower heads amongst the leaves. Here the flowers are blue brodeia, pelargoniums and pink chrysanthemums.

Home-made jam and buttered bread deserves a basket of summery flowers beside the silver tea pot (above). Alpine strawberries, phlox, roses, jasmine, pelargonium, geum and hydrangeas are all offset in a shallow, rustic basket.

Facing page top: a romantic dinner in the garden on a warm summer evening. a densely packed, tall-stemmed glass of old fashioned roses adds scent, colour and texture to a beautiful setting.

Facing page bottom: a formal dinner party with elegant china, sparkling glass and shining silver. A soft and pretty arrangement in restrained shades of apricot and pink.is set in the centre of the table. The flowers are kept low so as not to impede conversation.

CHAPTER 3

PERFECT PARTIES

*P*ARTIES ARE USUALLY HELD to celebrate something and flowers are a perfect way to put the message across. The trick is to make the most of the flowers that you can afford to give the maximum impact. You will have to choose a colour scheme to blend with where a party is being held, and you should also consider the lighting that will be used and the time of the celebration; for example, a hotel entirely artificially lit will need different treatment from a daylit marquee.

When there is a large group of people flowers will need to be kept high if they are to provide any kind of impact. If there are tables for food and drink then some flowers can be concentrated there, as well as on small individual tables if guests are going to sit down to eat. Buffet tables can look superb garlanded round the edges using ropes of foliage, while little sprigs or individual flowers can be pinned all over the cloths for a dramatic effect.

If there is a theme for a party then the flowers can obviously follow this through. A wedding anniversary might suggest a colour theme, a Halloween party would provide plenty of ideas. Outdoor summer parties, even if they are simple, spontaneous barbecues, can be a chance to use flowers imaginatively. Find suitably chunky, outdoor-type containers to begin with, as a garden is not the best place for fine crystal or porcelain. Clay

Facing page: a garden barbecue for a crowd. Colourful tubs of flowers and jugs of bright garden blooms among the food make a stunning display.

Above: a buffet party for a few good friends. The colour scheme is unusual and pretty. A pale blue and terracotta Madras cotton cloth is the starting point for the apricot and coral flowers, including protea, lilies, dahlias and roses.

Right: welcome guests to a party with a garland of dazzling flowers. Using a ready-made foam base, a wreath like this is in fact very easy to put together. Some of the flowers included here are clematis, marigolds, roses, geraniums, pelargoniums, sweet peas, geums and nasturtiums.

Top: floating candles, flower heads and petals make a simple and effective party decoration.

Above: a flower or two floating in a bowl of water makes an attractive finger bowl or place setting decoration.

flower pots would look good, or find a collection of old cans stripped of their labels or painted a bright colour. Baskets too can look pretty in a garden setting; sometimes one big display will have the most impact, such as a wheel-barrow filled with flowers and foliage. Remember that, if an outdoor party is being held in the evening, white and pale flowers seem to light up the dusk and show up much better than dense, deep colours such as red, so go for whites, creams, pale blues and light pinks for a night-time event.

A welcoming garland on a door is a lovely way to greet guests, as is one on a garden gate to show people that they have arrived at the right place. Similarly a ball of flowers hung from a door way or porch has a special event feel to it and gets people in the right mood from the start. If the party is in your own home, make sure any room that is likely to be used has some welcoming flowers in it and, wherever possible, choose scented varieties to add something more to the party feel.

A few perfect blooms floating in a shallow bowl takes seconds to put together yet adds a luxurious and very special touch to a table. An iris, a sweet pea and a tiny piece of polemonium float with a few scented geranium leaves in a cut glass bowl.

A wedding reception held in a marquee is a great opportunity to
create magnificent flower arrangements. The large pedestal
arrangement will stand inside the tent and the graceful little
arrangements will be placed on buffet tables amongst the food. While
keeping to a pink and white theme, many different flower varieties
have been used.

Above: a very special birthday and a fitting cake to celebrate it with. Heads of delicate golden alstroemeria are simply laid all round the cake base and are easily removed when it comes to cutting it. Fresh flowers are somehow very much more special than artificial ones on a celebration cake.

Left: single white rose heads and tiny Michaelmas daisies strewn round the edge of a christening cake, and a tiny bunch of flowers laid on top. A hint of blue is added by the lavender, forget-me-nots and chicory flower.

The use of this number of flowers in a single arrangement might seem extravagant normally, but a special occasion such as a party is a wonderful excuse for putting together one or two lavish and show-stopping vases.

A pumpkin lantern is the highlight of the Halloween party, but the
arrangement behind in warm glowing autumn colours is every bit as
spectacular. Clusters of rose hips and berries are mixed with garden
chrysanthemums and helichrysums.

CHAPTER 4

SPECIAL EVENTS

HROUGHOUT EVERYONE'S LIFE there are special days, such as weddings, christenings, anniversaries, birthdays. Flowers have always been part of these celebrations, having been used in all kinds of ways, from decorating the clothes and hair of a bride to garlanding a christening cake.

Whatever time of year a wedding is held there is always lavish use of flowers. In fact, the decorating of a church and reception venue plus the flowers for the bride and her entourage can become a substantial part of the wedding expenses. But ask any bride and she is likely to say that the flowers are so important she will have what she wants no matter what it costs. In recent years the part flowers play in a wedding seems to have grown in importance and there is no doubt that they linger in the memory.

Facing page top: a deep red colour scheme for a ruby wedding celebration. Red roses of course, and deep glowing dahlias, spray carnations and alstroemeria.

Facing page bottom: a long, low arrangement using peonies, pink lilies and chrysanthemums, softened by stems of grasses and gypsophila, the focal point of wedding decorations in a country church.

Above: a white and silver arrangement for a silver wedding anniversary. Lots of different grey and variegated leaves make a perfect background for elegant white miniature gladioli, dahlias and greeny-white chrysanthemums,

Right: warm, glowing yellow flowers fill a basket for a golden wedding anniversary celebration. Wheat and solidago form the basis, to which lilies, roses, dahlias and chrysanthemums have been added.

Above: a beautifully simple three-tiered wedding cake looks stunning decorated with fresh flowers. The flower heads can be put into place at the last minute and will last through the reception. Single cream-coloured roses and white spray carnations look beautifully bridal.

Facing page top: an informal basket of flowers for a country church wedding, used to decorate the old stone font. Pink roses, lilies, chrysanthemums and alstroemeria look soft and pretty mixed with gypsophila, grasses and pale green eucalyptus leaves.

Facing page bottom: the same classic wedding cake treated in a very different way. The emphasis this time is on the posy on the top tier. This can be made up ahead of time and put in position just before the reception. The bunch is made from beautiful, full, pale pink roses, scented white freesias and white spray carnations.

While professionals are usually called in there is no reason why anybody with a love of and interest in flowers could not manage to organise most of the flowers for a wedding. You will probably need a helper or two to fetch and carry, but these days, with a move to simpler arrangements and a country style of wedding decoration, the task isn't as daunting as it might seem.

A small, family christening is a wonderful chance to be creative with flowers, with perhaps an arrangement or two in the church plus some table decorations and a splendid, flower-decked cake. The traditional blue or pink theme seems to linger on when it comes to christenings, though you could choose a white or cream colour scheme if you preferred.

Anniversaries and birthdays are rather special too and, as well as bouquets of flowers as gifts, people love to receive ready-made arrangements. Try to include a person's favourite flower or colour and pick as many scented flowers as you can find. For presents such as these be really extravagant with ribbon and wrappings and take trouble over small details such as labels. Birthday gifts can be made extra special by attaching small posies of flowers to the box or wrappings, or adding a single, perfect bloom or corsage to be used once the present has been unwrapped. In this chapter there are all kinds of ideas for weddings and anniversaries, and many of them are easy enough for anyone to try. It is immensely satisfying to be part of making a special occasion even more special.

A basket of flowers and a head circlet for a beautiful bridesmaid. Deep coral spray carnations have been used with creamy yellow freesias. The gypsophila is used to fill and soften the spaces between flowers, while a peach ribbon gives the perfect finishing touch.

A classically simple bride's bouquet. The bold shapes of the flowers
have been left uncluttered by foliage or fillers. Speckled white lilies
have been put with rich cream roses, apricot roses and long stems of
pure white bridal gladioli. A bunch like this does not need to be wired
unless the stems become too clumsy to make a neat handle. Ribbons
are a matter of taste and will depend on the style of dress that
the bride wears.

Facing page: slightly different sets of flowers for a pair of bridesmaids. The thickly clustered, heavy roses suit the older child with long hair, while the more open circlet looks sweet on a mass of blonde curls.

Above: creamy yellow and apricot roses are mixed with the fresh green of molucella in the circlet and posy.

Above right: gypsophila is added to give a daintier version of the same theme. Apricot spray carnations are added to the roses too.

Right: a long-stemmed glass candle holder makes a perfect vase for a sweet, pretty arrangement for a christening tea party. Pink roses and fragrant sweet peas are used with single chrysanthemums and Michaelmas daisies.

C H A P T E R   5

SEASONAL CELEBRATIONS

S WELL AS VERY PERSONAL CELEBRATIONS which happen in every family there are, of course, annual seasonal festivities. For the average city dweller these days it's often not that obvious which season is which in terms of weather, and unless you live near green spaces the changing pattern of the year is hardly noticeable. But every year people celebrate Christmas or Easter, and in the country, harvest time is still celebrated. Each of these feasts and holidays has connections with flowers, and every country has different floral traditions and special decorations particular to each event.

Flowers are scarce in the wild at Christmas in northern countries, so evergreen leaves and branches are brought indoors and nature's own 'decorations' are added — bright berries, pine cones and seed heads. Nowadays we add glitter and gloss with artificial decorations and, if we can afford them, buy many different flowers at Christmas time, even forced spring bulbs. There's no doubt, though, that the traditional things look best and people still like their sprigs of mistletoe and branches of holly.

Days such as Valentine's Day and Mother's Day have almost lost their meaning in a mass of cards and commercialism, but still

Facing page: the house awaits Christmas in a warm glow of colour from firelight and decorations. The traditional mixes happily with the modern and the magic is the same as it has always been.

Above: a tartan ribbon and a restrained bunch of glossy evergreen leaves with a few brilliant artificial berries add colour to a ready-made wreath. This would look equally good as a welcoming wreath on the door.

Tiny kumquat oranges spiked onto short lengths of wire add the colour to this dish of evergreen foliage and long, slim flower candles (left). Little spotted bows add a light-hearted touch. To create this arrangement, cut a block of floral foam to cover the dish and push leaves, candles and wires straight into it. Tape the foam securely to the dish to prevent everything from slipping.

Above: a bank of red and cream poinsettias makes a stunning display against the dark fire surround. Bare twigs and evergreen leaves have been painted silver to add sparkle, and tiny red fabric bows add the finishing touch. The poinsettias can simply be stood in their pots close together in the hearth, while the twigs and fir branches are contained in the grate.

Deep green evergreen foliage is traditional and always right. It needs the simplest decorations added to it so as not to take away from its freshness and colour. Facing page top: foliage with a few glossy berries and some pine cones added and, of course, a big cheerful red bow.

Facing page bottom: a basket brimming with good things: tiny wrapped presents, red roses, lighted candles and sprigs of gypsophila which look like frosted snowflakes.

flowers are by far the most popular way of celebrating both these occasions. A small posy of flowers picked by a child is still the most touching present a mother can receive, and who can resist a glamorous bouquet of red roses, even if it does seem a bit corny.

Easter heralds a re-birth of the natural world and, though it can fall when the ground is cold and the weather wintery, there is still an optimism in the air that spring is on its way. There are always wonderful spring flowers to be found, even if they have been grown under glass and it is a splendid chance to fill your house with the fresh yellows and greens of this time of year. Children are fascinated by what appear to be dead twigs opening out into life, so cut a few stems of shrubs and trees and bring them indoors to watch the soft, new leaves unfold. Use cardboard Easter eggs as unusual and pretty containers for flowers, or make tiny table decorations with real egg shells filled with very small spring flowers such as violets, primroses and all the delicate miniature bulbs such as scillas, iris, crocus and grape hyacinth.

Nuts in their shells are plentiful at Christmas and, along with glass balls and tartan bows, are used as a basis for this table garland (right).

Below: floating candles and silver tree decorations in a frame of evergreen leaves.

*The kitchen gets decorated too in this country farmhouse. Mistletoe is
a must, along with berries, crab apples and branches of greenery.*

The warmth of wood in this cottage kitchen (left) makes the perfect background for swags of fir and pine cones. Bold red poinsettias come ready-made as a Christmas decoration.

Above: an ambitious Christmas decoration for the corner of a room. Its basis is a tall wooden pillar supporting a candle. Gilded pine cones are twined on wires around the pedestal and arrangements of evergreen foliage and scarlet carnations are attached at the top and base.

Right: a fairy-tale Christmas tree in a single colour theme of silver. A natural tree has been decorated with garlands, chains and candle lights which sparkle and glow. Limiting the colours used on a tree usually results in a more sophisticated effect than would be achieved with multi-coloured decorations.

Below: a very simple but beautifully effective decoration made in a small wooden bowl. Sprigs of fir encircle a gold pillar candle and rich, velvety-red anemones add colour and warmth. A row of these would look lovely running the length of a dining table, or at each place setting for a Christmas meal.

Above: trails of ivy decorate a mantel shelf, together with shiny, red artificial apples and a centre swag of berries and ivy blossoms. Posies of red roses decorate the top of the shelf.

A garland (left) made on a foam base can be used flat as a table decoration or hung on a door or wall. Fir forms the basis of the garland, interleaved with a few sprigs of silver variegated eunonymous and studded with natural berries, rose hips and scarlet anemones.

St Valentine's Day is a marvellous opportunity to be totally romantic
and create a decoration or present in true Victorian style. A heart-
shaped basket is here filled with fragrant white lilac, single white daisy
chrysanthemums surrounding apricot carnations and
yellow rose buds.

The same basket containing a quite different colour scheme. Lilac
again edges the basket while red rosebuds fill the centre. The basket is
first filled with damp floral foam and the flower stems are cut very
short and packed in very tightly to make a solid area of colour
and texture.

Facing page: spring flowers decorate a church on Easter Sunday. Yellow and green seem to symbolise a new year of growth, and flowers such as primroses and daffodils have a simplicity and charm not found in the later summer blooms.

Above: pollen-laden pussy willow catkins and wild daffodils in a moss-lined basket.

Above right: traditional Easter simnel cake decorated with a bunch of primroses – a beautiful spring picture.

Right: pheasant eye narcissi have the sweetest smell to fill a church at Easter. Yellow forsythia is one of the earliest shrubs to bloom and almost everyone has daffodils in their gardens to provide for the decorations.

Once a year the Roman Catholic cathedral in Arundel, West Sussex, is decorated with a carpet of flowers (above). Running the full length of the nave, this beautiful display attracts many visitors.

Hundreds of flower heads are needed to make the elaborate designs, but there is no shortage of flowers or willing local helpers (above right) to strip the chrysanthemum heads from their stems.

The designs are first chalked out onto a dark background, then laboriously filled in with evergreen leaves and all the different coloured flowers. Slowly the patterns emerge (right), and the floor becomes a living carpet.

Mothering Sunday is more commonly known as Mothers' Day now, but the tradition of children giving posies of flowers to their mothers remains. The most beautiful gift is a bunch of tiny spring flowers from the garden, and this one (left) includes grape hyacinths, primroses, wallflowers, sweet violets and white pulmonaria. The paper doiley makes a lacy collar to complete the gift.

Right: an Easter table decoration that would be fun for children to make. Cleaned out egg shells make tiny containers for miniature flowers from the garden. Add a real nest, a fluffy chick and a few sugar eggs and stand everything inamongst some yellow straw or hay. The egg shells are supported by pieces of egg box, secured to the plate with plasticine if neccessary.

The ancient custom of well-dressing is probably of Celtic origin and involves large wooden boards being decorated with elaborate designs made from flower petals and set up at local wells. The art is still practised in Derbyshire, where about thirty towns and villages participate in the rite. Well-dressing begins in spring and carries on through to summer, usually falling on days of religious significance. The designs reflect Biblical themes and are made from thousands of flowers, seeds, cones, leaves and grains. Wet clay is spread onto wet wooden boards which have previously been soaked for about two weeks in the local river or pond. It is not untypical for eighty or more local people to help with the dressing of one well. Here, the heavy boards are being taken from the Bradford River at Youlgreave after soaking.

Top: very soft, wet clay mixed with salt is flung onto the wet boards and smoothed over to an even thickness of half an inch. Here at Youlgreave the process is done on the banks of the river.

After the design has been traced onto the clay, the outlines of the patterns are marked with small black alder cones for definition and infilled painstakingly with petals (top right).

Above left: the town band marches through the streets of Youlgreave on the way to the well blessing.

An open-air blessing service is held at each well. Above: the blessing at Coldwell in Youlgreave.

Left: the finished well at Coldwell, Youlgreave, in June.

Wherever possible, only natural materials are used to provide the colour for the boards. This is easier to do in the summer, when there are plenty of flowers available. Some villages dress their wells in early spring when it is harder to find quantities of colourful petals.

The well at Holywell Lane in Youlgreave (above and left) is dressed from the Saturday nearest to St John the Baptist Day, which falls on June 24.

Facing page: the enormous and very elaborate Hand's Well at Tissington.

Above: the Children's Well at Tissington.

Above right: Hall Well at Tissington.

Yew Tree Well (right) is one of six wells decorated at Tissington on Ascension Day.

Autumn is a rich and fruitful
time for the flower arranger.
Make use of decorative
pumpkins, gourds and fruit and
combine them with the warm,
glowing colours of late
chrysanthemums (above).

Left: a golden arrangement for
an autumn harvest festival.
Chrysanthemums,
helichrysums and alstroemeria
stand simply in a glass tank.
The gourds, nuts and pumpkins
add colour and
interesting shapes.

C H A P T E R   6

FRAGRANCE FIRST

OR CENTURIES we have tried to capture and copy the scents of flowers. The range is enormous and flower fragrances include every type of smell we can describe, though few languages contain the words needed to do this properly. The ability to detect and enjoy fragrance varies enormously from person to person, and is influenced by age, sex, and health, but most of us can recognise the more common flower scents and appreciate them.

It always seems a little sad when flowers that we expect to produce a wonderfully rich scent have nothing at all. Unfortunately many flowers grown commercially have been highly bred and hybridized to produce long-lasting, stiff-stemmed and uniform blooms. These plants are then grown fast under cover in less than natural surroundings and, like battery hens,

produce something realms away from the original product. To get maximum scent in your flowers you really need to grow your own, choosing old-fashioned varieties as close to the original species as possible.

Some of the simplest and most unsophisticated flowers have the best scents, although many plants which need tropical conditions have some of the headiest and most exotic fragrances, such as gardenias, tuberoses, and stephanotis. If your taste is for simpler scents then go for the country-garden flowers such as honeysuckle, sweet peas, pinks and hyacinths. Old-fashioned climbing and shrub roses generally have stronger-smelling flowers than most of the newer rose hybrids, which are often very disappointing. These old roses are not as stiff and formal as, say, hybrid tea roses, and therefore make very different styles of

Some of the finest fragrances are to be found in the lily family.
Arrange lilies simply (facing page) and just enjoy their perfect scent.

Above: an early summer posy of mixed garden and florist flowers.
The delicate bells of lily of the valley have an incomparable scent, and
honeysuckle fragrance is warm and sweet. An antique glass goblet
makes a perfect vase.

arrangements. You will have to decide whether scent or form is most important to you when deciding which roses to grow.

Some flowers, such as lavender, retain their scent when dried, so it is possible to make dried flower arrangements bearing this in mind and choosing the most scented flowers you can find. Certain cut flowers have been grown commercially because they are highly scented, although they are not particularly beautiful or useful flowers in themselves.

Small bunches of sweet violets are still available just as they were in Victorian times when they were sold by pavement flower sellers. Their damp woodland smell is like nothing else. Freesias are not particularly beautiful flowers, but their scent is fresh and exhilarating. Sadly, some of the larger, new varieties of freesia seem to have all but lost their scent. Let's hope this doesn't go the way of the scent of the florists' rose.

During winter and early spring many garden shrubs and plants produce flowers with beautiful scents. Gather everything you can find and group them in small glass vases to enjoy. Left: iris, winter honeysuckle, viburnum, mahonia, tiny violets and jasmine, and pink and blue pulmonaria flowers.

Above: sweet violets in a tiny, white porcelain cornucopia.

A glorious summer garland of scented flowers. Full blown, old-fashioned shrub roses are mixed with sweet peas and rich pink clematis. Poppy seed heads and astrantia flowers add an unexpected touch, and glossy green choisya leaves make the perfect foil.

Above: sweet peas fill a glass jug and scent the whole room with their marvellous fragrance. One of the most useful flowers to grow for picking, every gardener should find some room for a few plants.

Freesias (left) are available all the year round and their scent is rich and exotic. Just a few stems will fill a room with fragrance. They can be used with other flowers or left plain and simple.

Facing page top: a spring basket of pink and white hyacinths. Their scent is gentle and delicious and very evocative of spring.

Facing page bottom: a romantic corsage for a wedding guest made from white miniature gladioli, pale pink roses, sweet peas and a sprig of honeysuckle.

Above: a pretty Victorian basket filled with a pot pourri of rose petals and summer flowers. To make the whole thing more decorative, dried flower heads have been wired around the edge of the basket. Pink peonies, helichrysums, larkspur and bronzy-cream hydrangea florets make the perfect materials for the flowery edging.

C H A P T E R 7

HERBS AS FLOWERS

*T*HERE IS ONE GROUP of plants in the garden which have a special significance. Herbs belong to the useful category of leaves and flowers which in the past have been used for food and medicine. Many plants are edible and thousands have special properties for use against illness and disease; the varieties which we grow today as herbs have been well proven through the years. Often these plants are very decorative in their own right, though some are simply plain and insignificant. Many of them have scented and aromatic foliage and flowers and all are good garden plants, either grown together in a traditional herb garden or simply put more naturally amongst other plants and flowers.

Herbs fall into various categories, and for all kinds you will probably need to grow your own if you want to use them as decorations. Cut herbs are available fresh these days, but they are definitely only suitable for using in food. A few herb varieties are grown and sold as cut flowers and it may be that, in the next few years, more will become commonly available. Dill, caraway and other umbellifers are sold in florist shops as their flowers are long lasting and very pretty, similar to the hedgerow's Queen Anne's Lace.

Dill is one of a group of annual herbs quickly grown from a spring sowing of seed. Try growing borage, marigold, basil and summer savory too. Perennial herbs include rosemary, mint,

Facing page: a field of deep purple lavender. This old and well-loved
plant has been used for centuries in medicines, herbal remedies,
cooking and throughout the household for its fresh, astringent scent.

Above: little posies of fresh herbs from the garden, the most delightful
gift or instant bouquet. Several bunches in a bowl in the kitchen look
pretty and might provide inspiration for the cook. Many herbs have
very pretty flowers, often in shades of pink and mauve, and the leaves
come in many different shapes and various tones of green.

Above: the blueish-green colour of rue and its pretty, ferny leaf shape makes it a very attractive basis for a summery white and green garland. Mixed with it are sweet peas, hydrangea florets, jasmine, hebe and astrantia. Touches of lime green are provided by Alchemilla mollis.

lovage, chives and feverfew. Quite a few of our commonest herbs are sub-shrubs coming originally from a Mediterranean climate, including thymes, sages and artemisias. They all thrive in well-drained, sunny positions, and though they don't mind cold during the winter they hate to be sitting in cold, water-logged soil.

There are a few biennial herbs too, such as angelica and caraway. Many herbs come into flower in early summer and their insignificant but subtly pretty flowers are well worth picking to use in arrangements and posies. A little bunch of mixed flowering herbs makes a lovely decorative and practical present to take to a friend, particularly one who enjoys cooking. The posy can be put in the kitchen and sprigs used when needed to flavour a recipe.

A very pretty and useful herb to grow is the golden form of feverfew. This plant has lovely, lime green foliage, which stays fresh and sunny all year, and in the summer the plant is covered in small, white, daisy flowers with yellow centres. Feverfew makes a very useful filler in arrangements and adds an attractive highlight to all kinds of colour schemes.

Facing page top: freshly gathered lavender made into old-fashioned lavender bottles. These are dried and used amongst stored clothes or linen to keep the fabric smelling sweet and free of moths. Nowadays they are more often used decoratively, with pot pourri, for example.

Facing page bottom: a glowing, deep pink semi-double rose. The rose has played an important part in herbal remedies and in the kitchen for centuries. One variety, Rosa officinalis, is also known as the apothecary's rose.

Marigolds and nasturtiums (right) are both culinary flowers, being used to add flavour and spiciness to food. Together here, and mixed with fennel flowers, Alchemilla mollis and yellow loosestrife, they make a delightful countrified garland. The sprigs of golden marjoram leaves add a sweet scent and brilliant green colour.

Below: a mixture of herbs, showing their great variety of leaf shapes and colours and proving how decoratively they can be arranged together. This basket includes sprigs of sweet woodruff, sweetbriar rose, golden feverfew, variegated mint, rosemary, sweet cicely, bronze fennel, blue rue, golden marjoram, chive flowers, lovage, Alchemilla mollis and salad burnet. Wild strawberry flowers, purple sage and common thyme complete the bouquet.

A sunny kitchen windowsill is the perfect home for a terracotta jug
full of garden herbs. Lemon balm, purple sage and variegated mint
leaves make a background for marigolds, lavender, feverfew flowers
and a bunch of lavender.

CHAPTER 8

FLOWERS AS FOOD

*T*HE IDEA OF USING FLOWERS in food seems strange to many people, but it is really no different from eating the leaves, stems or roots of plants, which we do without a second thought. There are certainly some flowers which should never be eaten, and others which will do you no harm but will taste vile, but this is the same for leaves, and you simply need to know the flowers which are perfectly safe and delicious to eat. Flowers are often used to decorate food and not meant to be eaten; through the eighteenth and nineteenth centuries there were many recipes for elaborate puddings smothered with fern leaves, flower heads and crystallised stems

and seeds. We use flowers decoratively on and around celebratory cakes and perhaps to embellish a special gateau, but it is only recently that we have looked back to the past and copied the idea of using flowers as an important part of a recipe.

Before modern methods of preservation were available, finding ways of keeping summer produce through to the winter was important and any ingredient which added the taste of summer to dull winter meals was a blessing. Flowers were steeped in drinks to give these flavour, and cooked in jams and preserves. Rose petals make a delicate and delicious jelly, as do many of the scented geranium varieties. Summer salads can be given a new

Facing page: freshly picked heads of pink sweet peas and deep blue cornflowers form natural decoration on an iced sponge cake for afternoon tea in the garden. These are not designed to be eaten, but simply to look delightful until the cake is cut.

Above: a pyramid of fruit in a compotier, made to look more glamorous with the addition of glossy leaves and brilliant orangey red alstroemeria flower heads.

Left: primroses and violets crystallised with gum arabic and caster sugar are made in the spring and kept to decorate special cakes throughout the year. As well as looking pretty, they are edible and quite delicious. For extra flavour, use orange flower water to dissolve the powdered gum arabic.

For long, cool summer drinks, encapsulate tiny flowers in ice cubes (above). Choose colourful and edible varieties such as borage flowers. Half-fill the ice-cube mould, then add the flower and a little more water. Freeze this and then top up with the rest of the water – otherwise the flowers tend to float to the top of the cube.

Borage flowers and leaves (left) are traditionally used to add their faint cucumber flavour to a gin sling or Pimm's cocktail. They also look ravishingly pretty in this delicious summer drink. Borage is an annual plant which grows very easily from seed sown in the spring.

Facing page: the ultimate summer salad, consisting of marigolds, nasturtiums and borage flowers mixed with salad leaves.

lease of life if you use many different salad leaves, adding edible petals to give colour and flavour. The petals of pot marigold add a slightly spicey flavour, while nasturtiums give a hot, peppery taste as well as adding vitamin C. Borage flowers are traditionally added to wine cups and summer drinks — the brilliant blue, star-like flowers are said to revive the spirits and make people cheerful. The whole of the borage plant has the slight aroma and taste of cucumber.

If you use flowers and petals as a decoration on food, do be subtle and understated and never smother the food with blossoms. A slight scattering of petals across the surface of a pudding or just one perfect bloom alongside a cake or dessert will have more effect than a whole bunch of flowers. Use flowers to enhance or bring out a colour in a particular dish or to emphasise a style of cooking. One of the prettiest ways to use flowers is to encapsulate them in ice cubes for refreshing summer drinks. Be sure to use only those which are edible, such as rose petals and borage flowers.

CHAPTER 9

DRIED AND SILK FLOWERS

 LOWER ARRANGING, in one form or another, is as old as civilisation itself, and one can also safely assume that replicas of live flowers and plants have been with us for a very long time indeed. Certainly the early Egyptians made artificial flowers and leaves, and used them to adorn the human body as an expression of delight in beauty.

According to Chinese legend, the silk strands of silk worms were discovered about 2700 BC in a mulberry tree in the garden of the Emperor Huang-Ti. Whether or not this first silk was used to make flowers is by no means certain. What is certain, however, is that the Chinese created artificial flowers in one form or another very early in their development. Flowers, especially the lotus, which is of special significance in Buddhism, were doubtless fashioned in paper, silk and later in metal, sometimes gold, and were adorned with precious or semi-precious stones.

More recently, artificial flowers have been made from materials as diverse as taffeta, satin, lawn, velvet and, of course, plastics, as well as feathers, shells, wood, cork, enamelled metals, glass, china and porcelain.

In 1871 a census revealed that there were 4,886 persons, mainly women and young girls, employed in the manufacture of artificial flowers in Great Britain. The material used would have been fabric, dyed and cut to shape. Between 1871 and 1885 the value of artificial flowers imported into Great Britain peaked at

Facing page: a harvest of rich red and bronze hydrangea flowers, which dry beautifully for winter arrangements. Left with their stems in just a little water they will dry naturally in a few weeks.

Above: a soft green, cream and yellow colour scheme for a dried flower arrangement using many of the fluffy, small-scale filler materials which are so useful when working with dried flowers.

Left: arrangements using dried flowers in many different styles and shapes, from classic baskets to garlands, pyramids and swags. Floral foam designed for dried flowers can be cut to any shape you choose and is available in several ready-made shapes.

Top: tiny posies made from dried flowers, each surrounded by a delicate paper ruff and finished with a ribbon bow. They look sweet individually, and can be used to fill a shallow basket.

Above: a marvellous collection of dried decorations using home-grown helichrysums and many other plants. The round garlands are particularly pretty, and not difficult to make.

Facing page: an explosion of brilliant colour from a basket of straw-textured helichrysum daisies. These come in a vast range of glowing colours and are among the most useful flowers for dried arrangments.

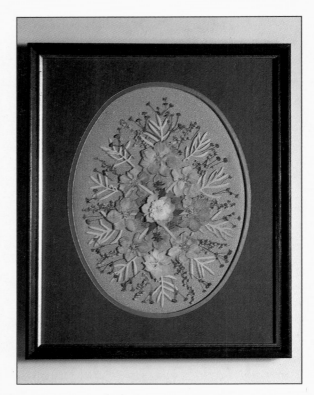

Beautiful pictures can be built up using pressed flowers and petals. Many varieties hold their colours well once pressed.

Pale pink and mauve larkspur flowers look stunning on a pale blue background with a tracery of silver foliage.

the figure of nearly £600,000, a staggering sum for those days. It is an even bigger industry today, and its classless product can be seen in the suburban semi and the baronial hall, for, as quality improves these 'fabulous fakes' are becoming very widely accepted.

Artificial flowers should not be confused with dried or preserved flowers, which are plants treated in a number of ways to retain their basic natural shape, colour and form, and in some instances also their fragrance. Artificial flowers are frequently referred to as 'Silks' or 'Polysilks' — a term which confirms the use of polyester-based fabrics in forming petals, leaves and buds. Polysilks are literally 'manufactured', usually on a mass production line operation. The exception to this method of production would be the more expensive, hand-wrapped specimens, which are sometimes made using pure silk.

The method of manufacture generally follows a number of processes or stages. The better quality ranges, which include plants as well as flowers, start life as photographs of live specimens, including photographs of a number of different sized petals and leaves so that variation in size and form may be achieved. An ingenious method of over-printing from the photograph is then applied to the long lengths of polyester fabric, which may have already been dyed or printed with the basic colour or shade. The fabric, now printed with a number of different sized petals or leaves, including veins and edge colour, is stretched over a cutting table. An accurately tooled cutter is then used to cut out the individual shapes. To achieve the required delicacy of shading and tone on better quality flowers, the desired concentrated

colour is dripped in measured quantities into the centre of the bloom, which is then subjected to high speed spinning. Centrifugal force then draws the colour outwards to create a natural looking finish to the flower.

Parallel to this process the 'stem', which determines the size and general shape and spread of the flower or plant, has been produced by a system of plastic injection moulding around a core of wire. The stem, usually green, can be bent into shape when creating an arrangement.

This stage forms not only the main stem but the side shoots to the individual blooms or heads of the flowers and, in the case of evergreen plants, also provides the web of veins for the leaf formation. Additional injection moulding of the base of the bloom, which fits onto the ends of the stems, completes the production process. However, in some species the individual petals are also wired to facilitate a more realistic arrangement. To give the petals and leaves texture they are subjected to a form of heat-crimping; this provides substance and a most realistic appearance and 'feel' to the finished product. The flowers and plants are then flat-packed into boxes ready for distribution.

It is interesting to note that up to this day the Chinese are still in the forefront of the production of artificial flowers, and the vast majority of 'Polysilks' imported into many Western countries are manufactured in the Far East.

These more sophisticated methods of production mean that the range of species is increasing all the time and quality is improving. The better examples of Polysilks currently available from the more specialist outlets are a far cry from the plastic

Right: grey velvet in a pretty, oval wooden frame makes a beautiful background for sprays of white roses and their leaves. A simple, naturalistic arrangement like this looks particularly attractive as the flowers remain quite true to life after pressing.

Below: an exquisitely complicated picture built up using many different flowers. A whole season of garden flowers is here, starting with snowdrops and daffodils on through to pansies, poppies, roses and hardy geraniums. The colours are quite strong and true and give the picture great life and depth.

A child's straw hat makes a perfect base for a pretty dried flower
decoration. Bright helichrysums and helipterums are wired or glued
round the crown. The big red bow gives definition and a touch of fun.

A small circle of dried golden-yellow helichrysums, silvery sea lavender and yellow achillea, with some deep brown foliage added to provide contrast. A decoration like this can be constructed using a ready-made foam base or your own base made from straw.

Top: the busiest time of year for a nursery that specialises in growing dried flowers. Harvesting and bunching has to be done at exactly the right time for the highest quality results.

Above: giant poppy seed heads develop a beautiful greyish bloom and look magnificent arranged simply in a warm brown basket. Save the seed and sow it for next year's crop of poppies.

Above: soft lemons and greens in a low arrangement of dried flowers for an occasional table. Many varieties of grasses dry well and retain their various shades of green. Here Mimosa centaurea and helichrysums are mixed with grasses and foliage.

Facing page: peach and apricot statice and roses spill out from a shallow basket. Sprays of sea lavender and santolina flowers provide contrast.

daffodils that were once offered as free gifts with packets of soap powder.

Polysilks can never, however, equal the real thing, and to some, their use is almost anathema. Those holding this view should, perhaps, skip the rest of this chapter. To those with less decided opinions, many reasons can be put forward for considering the use of Polysilks. Whilst in no way disparaging the use of live cut flowers or flowering plants, there are some problems which can be overcome by buying artificial flowers. Good quality Polysilks are not cheap, but they can prove to be quite cost effective simply because they won't die on you. The lasting beauty of an attractive display is, in the long term, cheaper than repeated live replacements. It does not require the 'tender loving care' of changing the water and cutting back the stems and the associated re-arranging that this entails. Also, they are not susceptible to cold draughts, excessive heat or dryness or lack of light. Polysilks are a good idea for busy people who are short on time, as well as those who might not possess the inclination or the skill required to create an attractive display of live flowers.

Few pleasures can be more satisfying than picking a bunch of flowers from the garden and arranging them in a favourite vase or pot. But not all of us have gardens and, for the busy flat-dweller, the use of artificial flowers can give a great deal of pleasure.

Another point in favour of Polysilks is that they can be used to most dramatic effect to create 'fantasy' arrangements. There are many artificial 'exotics' available, not necessarily replicas of live flowers or plants, but simply the product of the designer's imagination. Consider the stunning result, in the right location, of, say, a display of giant black poppies or a group of camelias in kingfisher blue! One point on colour when using Polysilks is that

you can achieve very accurate colour co-ordination when considering decor schemes, or complimentary arrangements with carpets, curtains and furnishing fabrics.

There are also, of course, many tropical species available, such as hibiscus, oleander, orchids, bird of paradise, bougainvillea and magnolia. One occasionally hears the argument raised that because Polysilks are so long-lasting one becomes bored with them. An answer to this is to buy a selection of artificial blooms and greenery and, when you get tired with one arrangement, alter it with flowers kept in reserve. Alternatively, simply put it in a box in a cupboard and bring it out again in six months time — a particularly useful trick if your live flowers start to droop just before an important dinner party. And just think — that poinsettia you bought for Christmas which is losing its petals by the New Year would still be 'alive and healthy' at Easter if it were a Polysilk.

The skill required to achieve an attractive display using artificial flowers is not greatly different from that needed for live flowers, but there are one or two points which would be useful to bear in mind. Firstly, you would require a pair of pliers or wire-cutters in place of scissors to cut stems to the required lengths. As a general rule, Polysilks tend to look better as an informal arrangement, although stylised displays can be quite effective in particular situations. We suggest that you do not mix them with live flowers, though they work extremely well with dried arrangements. Supplementing dried flowers with the wide choice of artificial foliages and fruits provides added interest.

The answer to the question 'where should you position your displays?' is simply 'anywhere you choose'. As previously mentioned, artificial arrangements are not prone to problems which effect live flowers, and it can be very satisfying and rewarding to place an attractive display in relatively inaccessible locations knowing you will not have to keep topping up the water or re-arranging it.

One important disadvantage of Polysilks is that underlighting or backlighting can ruin the effect. The polyester fabric becomes semi-translucent, the wired stems show through and, worst of all, the colour tends to become washed out and look faded. However, top lighting looks marvellous — any flower arrangement, live or artificial, will benefit from thoughtful lighting.

An important point on the art of arranging is that the blooms will, because they are wired, stay exactly where you want them to. However, try not to over-bend the stems as your arrangement will not look natural. The objective is, after all, to try and emulate Mother Nature in colour, form and texture.

Another advantage of artificial displays is that the choice of container is virtually limitless, and you do not have to consider whether or not the receptacle will leak. Obviously, ceramic pots or vases can be used, but so too can copper, brass or any other ferrous or non-ferrous metal containers. Equally, you can create attractive arrangements in basket-ware, rattan, cane, wooden, stone, terracotta, plastic, plaster, alabaster and marble containers. Glass containers can be used with the proviso that, if possible, a narrow-necked vase or bottle should be used as this will not require packing. It should also, preferably, be opaque or semi-opaque as the plain wired stems on Polysilks are a bit of a give-

Above: an antique chest brims with dried flowers in a glorious hall decoration, which will last through the whole winter. Red roses are the main material, together with trails of dried hops.

Below: rich mixtures of colour and texture resemble an old tapestry.

Above: warm oranges and reds
combine to echo the soft colours
of the antique eastern rug.
Roses and dahlias are arranged
with helichrysums and poppy
seed heads in a sturdy,
rectangular basket.

Left: brilliant jewel colours
from the dried helichrysums
warm a cool colour scheme in
an elegant dining room. The
colours glow particularly under
artificial light and the circle of
flowers makes a stunning
centrepiece to an antique
plate collection.

Above: a clever wall decoration made using part of a basket and
orange and yellow dried blooms. The eleagnus leaves have been
preserved in glycerine, which gives them a rich brown colour. The
trompe l'oeil effect is particularly pretty against the stained wooden
matchboarding wall.

Dried flower arrangements are all about texture and colour. Aim for a rich mixture of flowers (above) and use plenty of material.

Left: an unusual colour theme for a basket, chosen to echo the wall hanging fixed behind the flowers. Deep blue larkspur and sprigs of lavender are mixed with golden yellow marigolds, heads of achillea and small bunches of soft, greenish grasses. The poppy seed heads add shape and give definition to the whole arrangement.

*Semi-double white roses are used generously in this silk
arrangement in a simple pink and white
ceramic container.*

away and should not be left visible. With the exception of vases
or pots with a narrow neck, your container should be packed prior
to creating your display. One may use the ubiquitous floral foam,
but far cheaper and equally effective is left-over polystyrene
packaging, which can be broken down into pieces and pushed
firmly into the container, leaving a gap at the top which is then
dressed with ornamental grade 'Cambark', peat or just fine garden
soil if you so wish.

Whilst the packing should be firm and tight, care should be
taken not to over-stress the pot, especially if there are any small
cracks in it, or if you are using a fine piece of porcelain or an
expensive antique.

In conclusion, when considering using Polysilks one should
remember the old adage 'beware of cheap imitations'. They are
all imitations, the trick is to avoid the 'cheap'. Unfortunately, there
are quite a few cheap and nasty products around. The colours of
these are gaudy and unnatural, and they are frequently badly

made and often bear little resemblance to the flower or the plant
they purport to represent. This gives the artificial flower and plant
supplier an undeserved bad name, when in fact there is an
excellent range of beautiful and utterly convincing species
available. So shop around, and be prepared to pay that little bit
extra for good quality.

Right: yellow single spray chrysanthemums, looking pleasingly natural grouped in clusters on the stem. Arranged very simply on their own they make a sunny focal point for a city interior.

Below: soft yellow roses and rose buds mixed with smaller-scale roses and given an unexpected accent of bright sky blue. The whole arrangement is set off perfectly by the shiny brass container.

White silk flowers (right) with rich golden stamens have an almost Eastern appearance. The dramatic outlines of petals and leaves and the plain white vase.look just right against a very dark background.

Below: sprays of tiny white flowers like a single gypsophila mixed with camellia-type blossoms with deep golden stamens. The whole arrangement benefits from a dark background, which throws the flowers into relief.

Enormous and extravagant ,deep-red silk blooms tumble out of a
beautiful, silk-lined sewing box. Silk flowers are perfect for such
locations as there is no fear of spoiling heirlooms with splashes of
water or messy stems. The touches of white highlight the flowers and
separate the roses from each other. A few pieces of real fern add the
richness of natural green and succeed in adding to the illusion
of fresh flowers.

*Deep-golden, double yellow chrysanthemums glow in an old brass
container. Ideally suited to a dark and awkward position such as this
shelf on a bookcase, they look bright and sunny and, being made from
fabric, will last for months.*

Brass, copper and polished metal containers are ideal for silk flower
arrangements and can come to no harm. Containers which wouldn't
ever be suitable for fresh flowers, such as vases made from wood, or
old ceramics with cracks or chips, can be used for dried arrangements.

Right: peach roses combined with single white daisies, lightened by small sprays of peach and white flowers and arching blades of grass.

Below: the strong blue of cornflowers and exotically coloured grasses contrasts with single spray chrysanthemums and long spikes of larkspur.

Above: a beautiful, blue and white oval container filled with stems of blush white silk gardenias.

Left: the light, airy stems of silk aquilegia and stems of softly drooping blossom combine to give an effect like a Chinese painting in pale pinks and greens.

*Shades of gold and yellow in a silk arrangement using small-scale
flowers. An informal, natural feeling has been achieved by letting
stems droop loosely over the edge of the container. Touches of white
add freshness and definition.*

*Palest grey-mauve silk blooms arranged in a classic pale blue vase and
mixed with long-stemmed white roses. In this arrangement the foliage
has been made to appear as important as the flowers, and softly
arching grasses add fluidity to the overall shape.*

Above: rich-cerise, spiky-petalled silk chrysanthemums grouped into a shallow, round container and standing on a hall table. The foliage is a good glossy green.

Left: in summer, a fireplace is filled with a large basket of deep yellow chrysanthemums with a rich reddish centre. They will look cheerful in this location until winter comes and fires are lit once more.

A shining brass jug holds a bold mixture of red, white and blue. The
brilliant red poppies have been put with very realistic blue cornflowers
plus a few touches of white and some pretty silvery foliage.

Top: red, white and pink silk anemones and white gypsophila provide a simple windowsill arrangement. The simplicity of the shiny white vase lends great style to the arrangement.

Above: a thick mass of pink chrysanthemum blooms fills a pretty cane bedside table. Silk flowers are the perfect choice for bedrooms and guest rooms.

Facing page: the warm pine of a modern kitchen dresser makes a superb backdrop for a little brass container of single yellow chrysanthemums. Arranged quite loosely, they create the right impression for a kitchen setting.

CHAPTER 10

FLOWERS FOR GIFTS

*F*LOWERS ALWAYS MAKE perfect presents. Whether it is to say thank you or welcome, happy birthday or bon voyage, they always hit the right note. Even when flowers are sent in sympathy or when someone is very ill they manage to bring with them a message of hope for better times ahead and comfort for the present.

A big, cellophane-wrapped bouquet dripping bows and ribbons is great fun to be given but not such fun to do something with later unless the choice of flowers is imaginative and the quantities generous. Often the colours are badly chosen and once

the wrapping is off the bouquet all it contains are three or four roses, an iris or two and some carnations, with foliage for bulk. Trying to make an arrangement from this kind of choice would be difficult for even the best professional. If you want to give a bunch of flowers for a birthday, for example, either make a bouquet up from one type of flower or two in toning colours, such as a big bunch of pink roses or yellow lilies with cream roses. Alternatively, make a large-scale posy using bought or home-grown flowers which can simply be stood in a container after it has been received.

*Facing page: a bright, cheerful basket of flowers to give as a present.
Simple to make, it shows that a lot of thought and care has gone into
the gift, and, when the flowers are finished, the basket remains to
evoke a pleasant memory.*

*A glamorous sheaf of flowers (above) is always appreciated as a gift
for a special occasion. Choose pretty tissue or wrapping paper to
match the flowers, and complete the gift with ribbon and a carefully
chosen label. This bouquet is made up of gladioli, alstroemeria,
carnations, lilies and sweet peas.*

A posy makes a lovely present. It can be placed in a small vase just as
it is and enjoyed for several days. Above and overleaf: little posies
made from summer garden flowers. Choose a colour theme and
always include pretty leaves as a foil.

Facing page top: dainty fuchsias and pelargoniums with astrantia and
purple sage leaves.

Facing page bottom: sprigs of parsley complement the gleaming
colours of nasturtiums and marigolds.

192

Older people or those without time or energy to arrange their own flowers always appreciate a ready-made arrangement. You can make any size you like in floral foam taped to a plastic tray or bowl. Be sure to cover the base by keeping some of the flowers and foliage as low as possible. Gifts like these also make very good bedside or hospital arrangements, saving nurses or ward staff the trouble of finding vases and having to do the flowers themselves. Keep the arrangement small and neat, including a few special or favourite flowers and perhaps some sweetly scented ones for added interest.

Small baskets with handles make excellent containers for flowers as gifts, as, once the flowers are finished, they can be used over again for different arrangements or for quite another purpose. The handle also makes transporting the flowers easy and the whole thing can quickly be moved about. It is possible to buy small, ready-lined baskets for these types of arrangement — look for them in flower shops and florists' sundries suppliers.

If you are taking flowers with you to a dinner party it is good to have something which needs only the simplest treatment on arrival. Most hostesses hardly have time to start complicated arrangements before a meal, even though they might want everyone to enjoy the flowers, so take simple bunches of one type of flower, such as a big bunch of anemones or colourful ranunculus, which can quickly be put into a vase with no further fuss.

Above: wrapped presents finished off with a fresh flower head or tiny posy. Dried flowers can be used to create a longer lasting decoration. Here, brilliant anemones and one perfect red rose say so much more than any label could.

A carefully chosen mixture of flowers (right) makes a delightful posy to give as a present. One beautiful coral rose provides the centrepiece, surrounded by deep purple sage leaves, starry London pride flowers, polygonum spikes, pink spray carnations and pelargonium flowers. The gift is finished with a rich gold doiley to make it very special.

Much thought has gone into making this pretty heart-shaped basket
filled with simple garden flowers. Nodding aquilegia flowers have been
combined with saxifrage and snippets of pelargoniums and mauve
chive flowers. The flowers could be made into a posy and simply
carried in the basket or arranged straight into it using damp
floral foam.

A delicious bunch of mixed flowers to say thank you, or to bring as a gift at a dinner party. Deep purple irises are placed with pinks and sweet peas, alstroemeria and unusual, quilled petal chrysanthemums.

It is easy to put a small posy together in your hand. Flowers can be
mixed quite randomly or made into a pattern, of concentric circles
using flowers such as roses, for example. Choose one flower as your
central bloom and, holding it in one hand, add single flowers to it in a
circle. When you have finished, tie the stems together with ribbon,
string, or a rubber band, and add a paper frill if you wish. Here a
spring posy has been composed of purple aquilegia, yellow buttercups,
pink wallflower and variegated foliage.

CHAPTER 11

LIGHTING MATTERS

L IGHTING IS A COMPLEX subject and one which is quite difficult to master when it comes to planning how to light a home. We tend to be rather haphazard in how we approach lighting, often ending up with a compromise instead of the best solution. How a room is lit will influence the way in which we perceive it, such as whether certain architectural elements are more important than others, how the colours in the room strike us, and what good or bad points are obvious.

In the same way, flowers lit in different ways can take on several quite different appearances. General overhead lighting will give a clear but rather bland view of what is in front of us, while lit from one side flowers will appear dense and there will be more contrast between the shadowed and highlit areas. Lit entirely from beneath flowers take on a slightly weird and floating appearance, whereas a small spotlight pinpointed in one area of an arrangement would intensify colour and detail. If the light source came from behind the flowers (for example, if the arrangement stood in front of a bright window) the shape of the flowers would be thrown into relief, and colour and detail lost, producing a kind of silhouette. These examples give some idea of what can happen in extreme cases. Though during the day most rooms are lit naturally, at night artificial light takes over and you are more in control of the effects that you can achieve. Most arrangements look their best with a gentle, all-over light plus a

Facing page: side-lit from a window, the colours in a beautiful arrangement bring a patch of sunlight into the house.

stronger side light to bring out form and colour. Spotlights are certainly fun to play around with, especially if you have large spaces and grand-scale arrangements.

Candle light, though utterly romantic, doesn't help flowers. The light is yellow, which alters colours, and generally weak in intensity, so lots of detail and shape is lost. It's best to go for white or cream flowers which will glow under candle light, choosing something fragrant to counteract any loss of visual impact.

A good way of learning how to arrange lights and how best to use them for making the most of flowers is to look at stores and shop room settings which are well lit and focus attention on particular products.

Above: an all white arrangement stands out in a dark interior where deep colours would simply disappear.

Top: the gentle light from a bedside lamp highlights a fragrant
bowl of roses.

In a room with no natural light, choose shapes which are bold and
sculptural and silhouette well against a homogenous
background (above).

Facing page: dramatic spotlighting brings brilliant red orchids alive
against an old oak table top.

The all round natural daylight of a conservatory (facing page) brings the strong contrasts and light and shade of the outdoors. Light and airy sprays of gypsophila (above) need a solid, dark background to throw them into relief. Against too pale a wall they would simply melt into
the background.
Right: these alcove lights throw a subtle, warm light over the arrangement below. During the evening this effect will come fully into its own, making the flowers a focal point of
the room.

Window sills make good settings for flower arrangements, providing
gentle side light and usually reflected light, too, from painted
woodwork. Facing page top: rich pink gerbera daisies look clear and
elegant and the light sparkles in the glass bowl.

Lit from behind, delicate flowers and leaves look fresh and ethereal.
Facing page bottom: pale blue and mauve mixed with white to
complement the decorated jug. Aquilegias, cornflowers, veronica,
chives and white dicentra are arranged with white rose buds
and polemoniums.

Above: the strong shapes of ornamental chillies highlighted against a
cottage window. The silvery seed covers of honesty come alive with
the light and contrast with the heavy ears of wheat.

CHAPTER 12

DECORATIONS AND ACCESSORIES

F̶LOWERS DON'T HAVE TO BE STOOD in a container of water on a piece of furniture. For as long as people have been around, they have used decorations made from flowers to adorn themselves. The smallest child is fascinated to learn how to make daisy chains and hang them as necklaces, and for some a natural response on seeing one lovely bloom is to pick it and slot it into a button hole or tuck it amongst long hair.

Once picked and out of water a flower won't last very long, but these sort of instant decorations aren't meant to remain for more than a few hours — after which time the mood may have worn off. A full-blown pink rose will turn an ordinary black party dress into a stunning outfit, while a circlet of fresh flowers will turn any tiny bridesmaid into a fairy princess.

Hats have always been trimmed flamboyantly with flowers, feathers, ribbons and bows. It is a good idea to have a few basic hat shapes to which you can add fresh flowers as and when they are needed and fashions change. A plain, natural straw hat can be used for countless summer weddings and functions by changing its look and colour each time with different flowers. A single, many-petalled bloom such as a rose or peony can be pinned or stitched to the top edge or underside of a brim or fixed to a crown ribbon if there is one. A complete circle of smaller flowers looks pretty too, running right round the hat where brim and crown join. Keep other trimmings very simple on a hat with fresh flowers and don't add too many other bits and pieces to detract from the natural charm of the blooms.

Facing page: an elegant straw hat decorated for a summer wedding. Palest silk satin ribbon trims the crown and pink carnations are discreetly tucked around the bow. Use long dressmaker's pins to secure the stems to the hat.

Few men wear buttonholes these days except on formal suits at special functions. At one time men were quite adventurous with the variety of flower chosen, but now at weddings white roses or carnations are rather predictable. Why not try different colours and why not a few different flowers too?

Flowers used in this way can be made to last as long as possible if the cut ends of stems are bound with stem wrap to seal in moisture and prevent them drying out. At one time people used tiny, silver flasks filled with water to hold buttonholes and corsages, but few of us would go to all that trouble nowadays. The traditional corsage flower, the orchid, will probably last for several days out of water anyway, and even roses and carnations are very good tempered.

Above: a bridesmaid's posy for a little girl. Small and easy to carry, it is made from Doris pinks, annual gypsophila and lime green Alchemilla mollis flowers.

A smart French straw cloche simply and stunningly decorated with
one enormous crimson peony. The stem is pinned to the hat band and
will last for at least a summer's afternoon.

A more permanent decoration for a large, brimmed straw hat. This
time dried flowers have been wired round the crown to make a sunny
circle of blossoms that will last as long as you want them to.

The habit of wearing corsages is not as common as it once was, but it
is a lovely way of making an outfit special. Here, fragrant freesias are
mixed with love-in-a-mist and hebe.

Top left: a buttonhole made from a many-petalled, old-fashioned pink rose looks stylish on a dark suit.

Above: a posy of tiny blooms makes a pretty corsage for a deep green coat. Deep pink spray carnations are used with white miniature gladioli and starry London pride.

Top right: a classic red rosebud with a single leaf behind pinned to the lapel of a dinner suit.

Above: three yellow rosebuds backed with golden-edged ivy leaves on a smart pin-stripe suit.

The traditional wedding buttonhole is often made from a white carnation and a sprig of fern (left).

A lace-edged handkerchief used to back a bold corsage made from a
single red rosebud, a blue cornflower and the white flower heads of
Singapore orchids. The variegated foliage makes an unusual and
pretty addition. The stems are wrapped in special waterproof tape to
protect clothing and keep the flowers fresh.

An evening dress can take a more elaborate and exotic decoration than day clothes. *Above:* a pale pink scented lily with slightly opened buds combined with a cream freesia and the delicate butterfly flowers of an orchid. A similar spray of flowers could be used to decorate long hair or a chignon, or simply be pinned to a pretty evening handbag.

Below left: a pale pink rosebud against a smart grey morning suit, offset by a single sprig of fern leaf.

Below: a single spray carnation – smaller and more manageable to wear with a dinner jacket than a full-size carnation.

Making garlands is a pleasing and easy form of flower arranging.
Foam rings can be bought to use as bases for fresh flowers, and when
finished garlands can be used horizontally or vertically. Yellow
marigolds and achillea are here mixed with white daisies and feverfew
flowers and the whole ring is studded with blue annual cornflowers.

Begin a garland by covering the whole foam base loosely with the
filler, in this case Alchemilla mollis, then add the next smallest
component, such as the small purple double geranium shown here.
Work your way round the ring, spreading the materials evenly
throughout. Next add slightly larger pieces, such as these sweet peas,
stokesia, and small pieces of bluish green sedum. Add the final
touches – here spikes of lavender – throughout the garland and fill
any gaps where the base still shows through.

CHAPTER 13

USING FLOWERING PLANTS

Fl LOWERING PLANTS grown for indoors do not have to be used like their plainer cousins, the foliage houseplants. People very often treat flowering plants in rather unsympathetic ways and don't do them justice by simply shoving them on a windowsill, often still in the plastic pot they came in, and then forgetting all about them. You should really see flowering pot plants as flowers which can be mixed with other plants, used in groups and put into interesting containers. In winter a little collection of bright primula plants dropped into a shallow basket can look spectacular on a low table with all their brilliant, jewel colours mixed together. By comparison, one single pot sitting alone in a window looks pathetic and miserable.

Plant bulbs in the autumn for winter-flowering displays of narcissus, hyacinths and crocus and use all kinds of containers to make them more interesting. Blue hyacinths look beautiful in old blue-and-white china or plain lemon yellow pots, while daffodils would look good in dark green, glossy pots. If you don't have anything that looks suitable, plant bulbs in plain clay pots for a simple, natural effect.

In the spring, plant lily bulbs in groups of three or five in a pot to bring indoors just as they begin to flower. Many lilies have the most fabulous fragrance, are very easy to grow contained in pots, and will continue from year to year if you feed and water them after flowering and put them back outside. You can bring many plants in from the garden for short periods when they are in flower. Plants which prefer to live outside or under glass such as fuchsias will be fine for a week or so inside while they are looking their best.

Facing page: a mass of snowy white blossom on this hardy azalea almost completely covers the leaves. Each summer the plant is placed outdoors and then brought back inside to flower during the late winter. Hardy Japanese azaleas thrive more readily than the tender Indian varieties.

There are also some easily grown flowering pot plants such as schizanthus and cineraria which, from one sowing of seed, will produce dozens of plants, so you can afford to use them generously. If you do have just one flowering plant at any one time and it looks rather unimportant and thin, stand it in a group with foliage plants or even tuck it into a flower arrangement to get a bit more mileage out of it. Once it has finished flowering only keep it if you are sure that it is long lived and may re-flower under home conditions. Many flowering house plants, such as chrysanthemums and poinsettias, are grown in very artificial ways which ruin their chance of growing on in normal house conditions, so it is best to throw them out after flowering.

Pots of lilies (above) are so simple to grow and they make wonderful indoor decorations when they are in flower. Plant the bulbs in a sandy compost in the early spring and leave them outdoors until mid-summer, bringing them in for a few weeks when they are at their best. Feed the bulbs after flowering and they should provide flowers for several seasons.

Top: pure white primulas look cool and elegant planted in a French blue cache pot. Primulas are ideal plants for a cool room or porch as they do not like too much warmth.

Above: a very effective topiary tree made from small evergreen leaves pushed into a ball of damp foam fixed to a twig stem. Glossy rose hips are added for the finishing touch.

Facing page: brilliant mixed colours in a basket of primrose plants. Flowering in late winter and early spring, these plants help to brighten the house in what can be a dull season.

Many small, winter-flowering bulbs make lovely indoor decorations.
Plant bulbs for yourself or buy small pots with the flowers about to
open. A group of Iris reticulata looks fresh and natural surrounded
by a layer of moss in a neat, shiny basket.

Gerbera are commonly seen as long-stemmed cut flowers, but they are also grown as pot plants with shorter stems set amongst rich green foliage. A group of mixed gerbera looks stunning displayed in an old tin hat box standing on an oak window seat.

CHAPTER 14

IKEBANA

O ONE VISITING JAPAN can fail to recognise that flower arranging there is something different from what we are accustomed to in the West. In many public places — in the concourses of large railway stations, at conference centres, in the foyers of hotels, in galleries, museums, and department stores — there will be monumental displays incorporating tree trunks, stone, metal and driftwood as well as flowers, while at roadside shrines, in private homes and often in the most unexpected places you will see more modest arrangements.

In Japan flower arranging has long been seriously regarded both as an art and as a *do* (tao) or path leading to self-understanding. Before Buddhism reached Japan, people used to offer evergreen branches at Shinto shrines where the nature gods were worshipped. After the introduction of Buddhism in the 6th century A.D. flower offerings were made at Buddhist temples; the priests who arranged these offerings in vases on the altar being the first flower arrangers.

It was these men who developed the early styles of flower arranging and laid the foundations of the art. Schools of flower arranging were established in many temples in Kyoto, the old capital, some of which still flourish today, among the best-known being the Ikenobo school, the earliest school of ikebana, which has its headquarters at the Rokkakudo Temple, and the Saga school based at the Saga Temple.

The Japanese have a deep love of nature. Evidence of this is found in the *hanami*, excursions undertaken by the emperor and the court to view cherry blossoms in the spring, while in the

Space is an integral part of ikebana and is the source of the feeling of quiet and stillness that it gives to a viewer. Ikebana is usually created in situ so that it can be made in response to its surroundings. The finished arrangement, like this moribana using camellia branches and deep orange lilies, forms part of a larger design (facing page).

autumn there were expeditions to see the maples in their autumn glory. Such excursions retain their popularity in contemporary Japan, with quantities of *sake* (rice wine) being drunk at tables spread with red cloths set out under blossoming cherry trees or scarlet maples. Flower festivals, during which decorated wagons were drawn through the streets and exhibitions of flower arrangements displayed on the wide verandas of palace and temple buildings, were popular. The emperor and his courtiers took a lively interest in flower arrangement. During the 16th century the practice of ikebana spread among the aristocracy and was also taken up by the warrior class of *samurai*, who found flower arranging, like the tea ceremony, a means of relaxing after the excitement and challenge of battle.

Above: strong lines and clear colours hold a free-style arrangement, whose reflection forms part of the design, together. The flame-like crests of tall-stemmed Strelitizia regina and the sensuous creamy arums command attention, effectively dominating the potentially distracting background. Fatsia leaves, orange peppers and mauve sea lavender mask the kenzan and fill out the lower part.

In the 17th century the wealthy merchant class began to take an interest in ikebana, and the latter half of the 18th century saw schools being established in the dynamic commercial centres of Osaka and Edo (present-day Tokyo). Ikebana also became a required accomplishment for *geisha*, the highly trained class of professional women entertainers.

STYLES OF IKEBANA

SOME OF THE EARLY arrangements, like the *rikka* style, which symbolically represents a landscape, were very elaborate, having formalised rules governing the length and direction of the branches and the type of material that could be used. Rikka arrangements vary in size from around two to six feet. Later, simpler styles developed, partly in reaction to this and partly to suit changes in architecture and in the interior design of what became the traditional Japanese room.

The quiet and tranquil atmosphere of the traditional room is achieved by the use of natural materials and soft, neutral colours. *Tatami* mats covered with finely woven reeds make a clean, warm surface on the floor. Light is filtered through *shoji* paper screens on the windows and the pale ochre or mushroom-coloured walls are devoid of decoration. Furniture is kept to a minimum and ornament reserved for the *tokonoma*, a raised alcove in one corner of the room. In the alcove hangs a scroll with a painting or piece of beautiful calligraphy. Below this is a single ornament that, like the scroll, will be chosen and changed to suit the season or the occasion. In the tokonoma, or hanging from the post that forms one corner of it, is the flower arrangement.

Arrangements made for the tokonoma are seen only from the front, so the material leans forwards towards the viewer. This important characteristic of ikebana must be borne in mind when placing ikebana in a western home: space must be allowed for the resulting depth of the design. The focal point of the arrangement became the position from which it was viewed, with the material reaching forwards and upwards to this point. As a consequence a person experiences a sense of engagement when confronted with an ikebana arrangement.

Classical ikebana is either formal *(shin)*, semi-formal *(gyo)* or informal *(so)*. Formal arrangements use bronze, lacquer or highly glazed ceramic vases of classical Chinese design and stand on a wooden or lacquer base known as a *kadai*. Informal arrangements are made in ceramic vases with a more subdued or matt glaze, in bamboo containers or baskets.

One of the most popular classical arrangements is the *seika* or *shoka* style. Smaller than rikka, the style evolved towards the end of the 18th century, adapting some of the formality of rikka

This dramatic free-style composition, combining leggy, weathered drift oak with anthuriums and strelitzia leaves arranged in a large, shallow bowl, was inspired by the calligraphic painting on the wall beside it. The leaves, scarlet flowers and skilfully balanced wood reflect the colours and sweeping brushstrokes of the painting.

An old sake bottle holds a chabana made from a leafless medlar branch and a handful of tiny yellow chrysanthemums. Beside it, a spray of cotoneaster rests across a shallow plate, its scarlet berries accentuating the autumn mood. Modest seasonal material like this is typical of chabana, as arrangements made for the tea ceremony are called.

to the more austere Zen taste of the period. Some seika arrangements use only one type of material, such as aspidistra leaves, yew or iris; others combine two or more varieties of flowers and branches, but none use the complex variety of material found in rikka.

Nageire is an informal style that devoloped parallel to rikka, partly as a reaction to its complexity and rigid formality. *Nageirebana* literally means 'thrown in flowers'. These smaller arrangements emphasise the natural form of the branches and flowers and use simple ceramic and bamboo vases or baskets and natural objects such as gourds.

One of the most popular forms of nageire is *chabana*, flowers arranged for the tea ceremony. Tea drinking, introduced from China in the 8th century, was used by Zen monks to keep them awake during *zazen* (sitting meditation). Later, tea drinking was taken up by the aristocracy as an occasion for the display and appreciation of expensive and beautiful objects. In the 16th century the tea master Sen-no-Rikkyu reformed the tea rituals, developing a simple and moving ceremony that has changed little to this day. In keeping with this he created a simple style of flower arrangement using a minumum of material. For chabana, inconspicuous, unscented seasonal material is arranged in a rustic container.

DIFFERENCES BETWEEN IKEBANA AND WESTERN FLOWER ARRANGEMENTS

IKEBANA MAKES MUCH GREATER use of branches than western flower arrangement. Flowers are subsidiary and many classical styles use few flowers or else omit them entirely.

Line is of prime importance. Branches are trimmed to elucidate a natural line and shaped to create curving or angular lines that lend interest to the design.

Space is consciously incorporated into the design and this is responsible for the sense of calm generated by ikebana. The focal point lies outside the arrangement itself, being in fact the person viewing the arrangement, usually from a position about three feet in front of it. The material reaches forward towards this point and

A few last cherries cling to a branch and small white chrysanthemums gleam like early snowflakes in this nageire style chabana arrangement for late autumn. The design on the handsome dish suggests the cloud-streaked skies characteristic of this season, while the old, lacquered bamboo basket gleams like ripe chestnuts.

engages the viewer, as it were, in a dialogue. A western arrangement, where the focal point is usually a beautiful, centrally placed flower, is self-contained and self-sufficient. But ikebana responds to attention and each person finds in it their own meaning.

Ikebana, like most oriental art, is characterised by asymmetry. It also uses the yin and yang (Japanese *in* and *yo*) principle of the balancing of opposites; space balances mass, line balances form, dark colours balance bright ones and so on. Three principles that govern all ikebana were established early on. These are:

a) all the material reaches upwards following the natural movement of growth

b) each arrangement has three main lines which form a triangle

c) the material is arranged so that it emerges from a single point in the container.

The study of ikebana involves three things. First there are techniques to be mastered; the cutting and shaping of branches and flowers and the process of fixing them securely in the correct position. Secondly there is the theory to be learnt and the history

to be studied. Finally there is *do*, the philosophy, the journey of self discovery. These characteristics are common to all Japanese arts: *ju-do*, *ken-do* (the way of the sword), *cha-do* (the way of tea), *kyu-do* (the way of archery) as well as *ka-do* (the way of flowers). When people ask 'How long does it take to learn ikebana?' the answer is you can, with application, master the techniques known as *jutsu* and the book-learning *gaku* in a relatively short time, but *do* is a lifelong study.

MODERN IKEBANA

MODERN IKEBANA DEVELOPED after America intervened to force Japan to open her doors to western trade in 1867. The consequent influx of new ideas and contact with the west radically affected life in Japan. Many people adopted western dress, and western-style rooms were introduced in public buildings and private homes. The traditional ikebana styles were adapted to suit these settings and to include new plant materials and the exotic flowers now available. Women were encouraged to enter fields formerly reserved for men, and took up ikebana on a large scale. New

A classical seika arrangement made in a formal bronze vase known as a usubata. The flowers and branches are held in place by a kubari so that they emerge from a single central point in the vase's wide mouth. The three main lines are clearly defined. Note how the branches of yew chosen for the arrangement echo the main tree in the scroll painting. The whole arrangement stands on a simple black lacquer base or kadai.

An informal seika of spring blossom arranged in a double-mouthed
bamboo vase; the first and third branches emerge from the lower
mouth, the second one from the upper mouth. This second branch
sweeps low following the line of Mount Fuji in the scroll painting.
The vase has been placed slightly in front of the scroll so that the eye
travels across the blossom to the mountain beyond.

schools were founded, notably the Ohara school founded by Ushin Ohara in 1895, the Sogetsu school founded by Sofu Teshigahara in 1926, the Adachi school, which initiated correspondence courses in ikebana, and the Ichiyo school, which specialised in courses for foreigners.

Ohara was the first to use western material for ikebana. He also created the *moribana* style using a shallow, flat-bottomed container. This style rapidly gained wide popularity. Since then ikebana has continued to develop and some avant-garde styles using such unexpected materials as metal, plastic, fabric and paper seem more like sculpture than flower arrangement. Nevertheless the traditional styles remain popular. Exhibitions draw large crowds and the range and professionalism of books and magazines in Japan devoted exclusively to ikebana is proof of the vitality of the art.

THE SPREAD OF IKEBANA OUTSIDE JAPAN

IN 1889 JOSIAH CONDOR published *The Floral Art of Japan*, introducing ikebana to the west. Ikebana became much more widely known outside Japan after the Second World War. Many wives of army officers and diplomats stationed in Japan studied the art and spread their knowledge on returning to their own countries. Ikebana International, founded in 1956 and now having chapters in over fifty countries, provides a focus for ikebana activities worldwide.

IKEBANA EQUIPMENT AND TECHNIQUES

LIKE ALL ARTS and crafts, ikebana requires tools and equipment. There are also skills and techniques to be studied.

Moribana arrangements, the easiest style to master, are made in a shallow, flat-bottomed container using a *kenzan* or strong pinholder to support the flowers and branches. Pinholders made for western flower arrangement are usually neither strong enough nor heavy enough to support the branches used in ikebana. Branches are cut at an angle, pushed straight downwards onto the kenzan and then moved into position.

For nageire arrangements made in tall, cylindrical vases, a variety of *kubari* (supports cut from pieces of branch) are used to hold the material in place. Classical arrangements also use various kubari to support the material. Branches are trimmed and shaped and then balanced in the container. Considerable practice is needed to achieve the required skill. Special scissors called *hasami*, which can cut both thick branches and thin stems, are used for ikebana. There are also saws, knives and syringes for more advanced work, special tools for cleaning and repairing kenzan, mats to protect the surface of costly vases and so on.

Ikebana is a fascinating study and the pleasure it gives, both to the practitioner and those who enjoy the results, richly rewards the effort involved.

Large arrangements are a common sight at exhibitions and in public places in Japan. Facing page: an arrangement, approximately five foot by twelve foot and six foot tall, set in London's 12th-century Temple Church and inspired by the 'Wedded Rocks' in Ise-Shima National Park. These two huge, sea-girt rocks, one of Japan's most famous sights, are linked by thick straw ropes in an annual ceremony. Here, twisted honeysuckle vine bridges the space between the symbolic arrangements. The large pot holds pine and rhododendron branches, bright pink azaleas and tiny yellow orchids. In the subordinate group, resting on an island of pink moss, purple irises, yellow jonquils and mauve eucalyptus are used. Driftwood and sea lavender anchor and fill out the composition.

Above: a flowing nageire arrangement in which skilfully trimmed Gaultheria shallon leads the eye up to the powerful bronze head and back again to the two asymmetrically-placed 'pincushions'. These Leucospermum cordifolium flowers pick up the highlights in the runner, made from an old Teke Turcoman camelbag. Small white chrysanthemums soften the neck of the stoneware vase.

Left: ikebana in a Western home – a shallow bowl containing yellow arums and pale anemones stands on an occasional table. Spotted laurel (Acuba japonica) masks the kenzan and bear grass adds delicate tracery to the elegant design. The arrangement looks perfectly at home in this setting.

Left: bare lilac branches and Mahonia japonica provide the three main lines in a substantial autumn arrangement. 'Fried egg' chrysanthemums and golden Singapore orchids gleam amid the sombre foliage and against the rough surface of the large Bizen vase.

Top: an autumn seika-style arrangement of big, creamy spider chrysanthemums in a large-handled 'peony' basket.

Above: a spring interpretation of the classical 'boat at rest' style using pussy willow and iris. The boat-shaped vase, made from a bamboo stem, rests on a pair of iron 'anchors'.

Tsuribana or hanging arrangements have both charm and, since they take up little room, practicality. Summer and autumn meet in this small arrangement in a hanging basket; the hips are already ripe on the climbing spray, but summer lingers in the warm apricot of the single rose.

Right: bold-leaved rhododendron and Fatsia japonica *used with rust and yellow spray chrysanthemums in a large, floor-standing pot. A niche in the wall above holds a small companion arrangement in which elegant scarlet euphorbia and berried cotoneaster reach forward from a small stoneware bottle. The colours were chosen to echo the painting on the adjacent wall.*

Below: a heavy, bulbous pot holds lichened branches salvaged after a gale and arranged in a strong diagonal line. The addition of two stems of pale amaryllis and a few pieces of rhododendron turns this it into a striking composition.

Above: a late summer arrangement that includes a greater richness of material than is usually found in ikebana: feathery astilbe, three varieties of chrysanthemum, azalea foliage, aspidistra leaves and hydrangeas in different stages. The inclusion of flowers at different stages of development, of withered or damaged leaves is characteristic of ikebana, reminding us of the ephemerality of all things.

Left: echinops and Strelitzia regina used with 'dancing lady' orchids and viburnum in a free-style arrangement in an abstract modern vase. In ikebana the container is much more than a mere water holder, instead forming an essential part of the composition. In free-style work, a bizarrely shaped or brightly coloured vase often provides the inspiration for the whole design.

The Publishers wish to thank the following individuals and organisations for their invaluable assistance in the production of this book:

For location facilities: Mr and Mrs J Burrows; the proprietors of Cannizaro House Hotel and Restaurant, West Side, Wimbledon Common, London SW19, Tel. 01-879 1464 (pp. 64, 67, 79, 88 bottom); Christ Church, Shamley Green, Surrey (pp. 134, 135 bottom); Mr and Mrs R Clark (and Basil the dog); Dr and Mrs Coen; Mr and Mrs John Collins; Mr and Mrs Clive Harvey (pp. 122, 125, 128, 130); Rear Admiral and Mrs Hill (pp. 233 bottom, 236, 237 bottom, 238 bottom); Mr and Mrs C Humber and Frances and Amelia Humber; Major and Mrs W James; Mr and Mrs Lucy of Petersham, Richmond; Alan R Mann, ARICS, London (pp. 225, 233 top, 237 top); Moyses Stevens Ltd, Florists, of 6 Bruton Street, London W1, Tel. 01-493 8171; the proprietors of Ston Easton Park, Chewton Mendip, Bath, Avon, Tel. 076 121 631 (pp. 69, 88 top, 90, 91 centre left); the proprietors of the Suntory Restaurant, 72/73 St James's Street, London SW1, Tel. 01-409 0201 (pp. 224, 227, 228, 230, 231, 234, 235, 238 top); the Temple Church, Middle Temple, London (p. 232); Peter Watkins, The Flower Stall, New Bond Street, London W1; Caroline Whyte (p. 118); and Janet Whyte, Chilmark, Wiltshire. The conservatory featured on pages 57, 91 top right and 96 is a cedarwood conservatory from the Cliveden Range of Hall's Traditional Conservatories Ltd, Church Road, Paddock Wood, Tonbridge, Kent, Tel. 089 283 4647.

For the provision of flowers, Spriggs Florists of Petworth, and Southdown Flowers of Yapton; for the loan and arrangements of silk flowers (Chapter 9), Annie Wimble and Abigail James-Bailey of Hennings (Acacia), 157 High Street, Rochester, Kent, Tel. 0634 403879; for the provision on loan of garden furniture, Secrett's Garden Centre, Milford; and for sundry flower-arranging accessories, Adams Paper Bag Co. Ltd of Chichester, West Sussex.

For providing material for the ikebana section (Chapter 14), The Ikebana Centre, 2nd Floor, 75 Kenton Street, London WC1, Tel. 01 833 2821/2; for carrying out the arrangements: Tricia Hill (pp. 227, 228, 223 bottom, 232, 234, 236, 237 bottom, 238 bottom) Angie Jameson (p. 233 top); Elizabeth Palmer (pp. 224, 225, 229, 232, 237 top, 238 top); and Sumie Takahashi (pp. 230, 231, 235); and for the use of their work in the photographs: Ian Auld (stoneware bottle, p. 233); Robert Clatworthy (sculpture, p. 233); Stanley Grimm (painting, p. 237); Janet Leach (stoneware bottles, p. 237); David Lloyd Jones (pot, p. 237) and Da Wu Tang (calligraphy, p. 227).

For additional arrangements: Dee Hine, Studio 4, Welsbach House, The Business Village, Broomhill Road, London SW18, Tel. 01 871 5146 (pp. 48, 52, 57, 64, 67, 68 top, 69, 72 top right and centre, 73, 74, 79, 81, 85 bottom, 86 bottom, 87 top, 88, 90, 91 top right, centre left and bottom, 94, 95 bottom right, 96 top, 97 bottom and top right, 202-205); Pat Lague (pp. 51 top left and top right, 92 top and bottom right, 129, 150 top); Jonathan Newdick (p170 bottom left); Jill Peeters (pp. 15, 62, 66 bottom, 70-72 top and bottom left, 75 bottom right, 78 top left and right, 82 top, 83, 86 top, 93, 95 top, 172 top); Hanni Penrose; and Joan Sutherland (pp. 87 bottom, 105 bottom).
Photographic assistant, Andrew Preston.

The Publishers also acknowledge with thanks the assistance given by His Grace the Duke of Norfolk and Father Anthony Whale (Administrator of Arundel Cathedral) in connection with the Corpus Christi Festival Carpet of Flowers, and by Stella Smart, Liz O'Brien and Ursula Taylor, who organise the creation of the Carpet at Arundel. They further thank Diane Harrison and Jim Evans of Youlgreave, Derbyshire for help in the photographing of the well-dressing ceremonies; and Vivian and Heather Taylor, of the Round House, Hatch Park, Loxhill, Godalming, Surrey, for the use of their garden for location facilities and for enabling photography to be undertaken in connection with the dried flower arrangements (pp. 30, 31, 36-39 top, 40-43 bottom, 45 top right, 163, 170 top, 174).